TO THE PEOPLE OF KASHMIR AND LADAKH.
THANK YOU FOR OPENING UP YOUR HOMES AND HEARTS TO ME,
AND FOR LETTING ME TELL YOUR STORIES AND SHARE YOUR RECIPES.
THIS BOOK IS FOR YOU, BY YOU.

ROMY GILL

ON THE HIMALAYAN TRAIL

PHOTOGRAPHY BY PORAS CHAUDHARY
AND MATT RUSSELL

RECIPES AND STORIES
FROM KASHMIR TO LADAKH

Hardie Grant
BOOKS

NASHTA

SNACKS & STARTERS

SEYUN

VEGETARIAN

MAAZ

MEAT

GAAD

FISH

MEETHA

DESSERTS

BAITH, CHAUTT & CHETIN

BREADS, RICE & CHUTNEYS

LADAKH

LEH

INTRODUCTION

KASHMIR THROUGH ROMY-TINTED LENSES

When I was a child in India, growing up in West Bengal, we were the first family on our street to get a television – an enormous black-and-white affair. Occasionally, we would invite neighbours and friends round to watch Bollywood movies. These were mostly filmed in Kashmir, the valley that was once the summer capital of the Mughals. With its stunningly beautiful lakes, snow-capped mountains and rolling meadows, it looked like paradise. It was partly these movies that were responsible for my fascination with this remote state, which straddles the Himalayas: one of the many, varied parts – each with their own distinct culture – that define the 'real India'. Growing up, Kashmir felt like a foreign country to me, and I longed to visit.

It wasn't just the lofty mountains and rolling valleys of the region that captured my imagination: the people and the food also had a huge part to play. This is all down to my father, Santokh Singh Sandhu, who at the young age of 16 had travelled to Burnpur in West Bengal to work in a steel plant. Here, he worked alongside people from across India: colleagues and friends, including several families from Kashmir, with whom we shared numerous meals and celebrations. It meant that I learned a huge amount about their culture, their religion, their food, their language and their values – and I learned even more when, just before winter came, Kashmiri traders would visit Burnpur with shawls, carpets, dried fruits and apples to sell. I have fond memories of my mother stocking up on purchases from Kashmiri people at this time of year, carefully bartering with them all before handing over any money.

Now, as a professional chef, Kashmir intrigues me for even more reasons: the various ways of living, speaking and feasting, and the different rituals ingrained into everyday life. With so much political uncertainty in the region, its cuisine and culture is increasingly difficult to access – but I strongly believe that it's a cuisine and culture that the world deserves to know more about.

In recent years, I've learned more and more about my home country through my travels to places like Leh, the Andaman and Nicobar Islands, Himachal, and many more. I've enjoyed the chance to eat, cook and learn about the food from each region, and then writing about it to share their incredible recipes and stories with a new audience. So, when I finally decided to travel to Kashmir, it would be no different: I was looking forward to enjoying the company of local Kashmiri people and seeing the region through their eyes.

I knew it wouldn't be an easy trip to plan. It was April 2021, and the COVID-19 pandemic had the world in its grip: every country had its own travel restrictions and its own regulations once you got there. Returning to India, when the country's ever-increasing case rates and deaths were making global headlines, was certainly a risk – but still, I was desperate to make this journey.

Great things never come from staying in your comfort zone. Anthony Bourdain once said, 'If I'm an advocate for anything, it's to move. As far as you can, as much as you can. Across the ocean, or simply across the river. [...] Walk in someone else's shoes, or at least eat their food – it's a plus for everybody.' So, I took the plunge and moved, spurred on by Bourdain's words, and my vision.

It was worth it. The scenery, the people, the traditions, the love – and, of course, the food – all came together to create a truly incredible experience for me in Kashmir. As a chef, the trip was an education, and I'm excited to share the Kashmiri recipes and techniques that I learned about here, in this book.

Kashmir, the northernmost region of India, is bordered by Pakistan to the north and west and China to the east. Unlike other places in India, Kashmir is largely untouched by foreign and domestic tourists, primarily because of its political situation.

In 1947, with the partition of India, both India and Pakistan tried to lay claim to Kashmir. Since then, fighting over the region has continued, and in 1990, the introduction of new powers for the military led to great government mistrust. As a result, over 70,000 Kashmiri Pandits fled the region, and continued to do so for the next decade. However, to me it was important to travel the parts unknown and to learn from them.

THE BASICS OF KASHMIRI CUISINE

Kashmiri cuisine draws its heritage from two different groups of people: the Pandits and Muslims. While there are differences between the two groups, there are also many similarities – most importantly, the fact that they both offer such a rich fusion of styles and flavours in their food. Both cuisines draw heavily on Central Asian, Afghan, Persian and Mughal styles of cooking, and both share an affinity for lamb-based dishes, cooked over a wood fire.

Perhaps the most surprising difference between Kashmiri Pandit and Muslim cuisines, though, is the fact that Pandits will cook without onions or garlic: two of the staples of the majority of Indian regional cuisine. Conversely, two ingredients that you will find in Kashmiri Pandit cuisine, but rarely in Kashmiri Muslim cuisine, are *hing* (asafoetida), and curd or yoghurt-based sauces.

Each group brings its own style of richness to the table, with a deliciously aromatic blend of spices, including cloves, cinnamon, green and black cardamom, and ground fennel and ginger. Some of my favourite traditional dishes include the Kashmiri Muslim *Rogan Josh* (page 98), with its rich, spicy gravy and vibrant colour and flavour, and the delicate and soft Pandit *Chaman Kaliya* (page 52): chunks of tender curd cheese cooked in a mild cardamom and fennel-scented sauce, perfect mopped up with a flatbread.

An interesting anecdote I was told on my travels was that, at one time, every single Kashmiri Pandit home in the plains had a professional cook in residence. It meant that Kashmiri Pandits were able to enjoy a feast fit for royals at every mealtime. The women of the households received culinary training from these highly creative cooks. Over time, however, the cost of living grew higher and higher, and the expense of such a rich diet proved too costly, and so the era of these professional cooks came to an end. Some migrated to different industries; some opened their own small restaurants; and some are still cooking on a contract basis, providing sumptuous feasts for weddings and other special occasions.

KASHMIRI CUISINE'S CROWNING GLORY

Throughout different states in India, we have regional *thalis*: a range of varied savoury dishes, all served together on a single platter. But these are a world away from the intricate Kashmiri feast, traditionally known as a *wazwan*. These traditional Kashmiri banquets are prepared and cooked by specially trained chefs known as *wazas*: descendants of master chefs who hailed from Central Asia at the start of the 15th century, during the reign of Timur. While I had experienced a variety of Kashmiri dishes and flavours when growing up in West Bengal, nothing could have prepared me for the experience of a lavish celebratory *wazwan*.

Throughout my travels in Kashmir, I was introduced to different ways of preparing and serving this amazing feast, which can feature anything from 26–36 courses, all cooked simultaneously in copper pots over fire, and starring a variety of meat dishes all from the same animal. It's such an elaborate meal that a number of the dishes are often cooked overnight, supervised by a *vasta waza* (head chef).

Dishes commonly found in a *wazwan* include *methi maaz* (lamb and fenugreek curry), *sheekh kebab*, *tabakh maaz* (Kashmiri lamb ribs), *rista* (saffron-flavoured meatball curry), *rogan josh*, *aab gosht* (a milk-based mutton curry) and *gostaba* (mutton meatballs in a yoghurt gravy).

Traditionally, Indian food is eaten with the hands and the *wazwan* is no exception. A *trami* – a circular copper platter – is brought to the table, laden with a mound of moulded rice, *sheekh kebabs*, and a plentiful supply of meat dishes, with yoghurt and other sides served separately. If you ever get the chance to enjoy a traditional Kashmiri *wazwan*, be sure to take a spoonful of yoghurt between every meat dish: not only will it help to cleanse your palate, but it will also help you to digest the these rich, stunning dishes.

Few foreign tourists visit Kashmir and get the chance to try these native dishes for themselves, but that doesn't mean you should miss out. I've brought these recipes back with me to share with you, in the hope that you discover some new favourites from this little-known part of India – and that, perhaps, you will be encouraged to visit this beautiful region one day.

BASIC SPICES & PREPARATIONS

KASHMIRI SPICES

While visiting the region and talking to many chefs and bloggers, I came to learn that in Kashmiri cuisine, there are particular spices that play a very important part in many dishes. These are chiefly ground ginger, ground fennel and red Kashmiri chilli powder, but also green and black cardamoms, cloves, cinnamon and mustard oil.

The older generations in the villages and the *wazas* (professional chefs) would always use a pestle and mortar to grind the spices, but among the younger generations, spice grinders are starting to be used. A pestle and mortar will give an authentic flavour and texture, but to save time, an electric grinder is absolutely fine.

Here is a quick rundown of the main spices you will find in Kashmiri cuisine and their various properties:

CARDAMOM: BLACK & GREEN

Green cardamoms enhance both sweet and savoury flavours. The aroma is strong, but mellow and fruity. It tastes very flowery and lemony, with a note of camphor. It is pungent, warm, bittersweet and very fresh. Used widely in spice blends, black cardamom pods are very different in flavour and texture to the green ones. Black cardamom is never used as a substitute for green cardamom. The seeds have a smoky aroma and taste of pine.

CINNAMON

Most Indian kitchens use cassia bark, as it has a stronger flavour, but in Kashmir people use proper cinnamon, which is more delicate.

CLOVES

Cloves are used whole in Kashmiri cooking, but sparingly, because they can easily overpower dishes. Their aroma is warm, with notes of pepper and camphor. The taste is very sharp, hot and bitter, and leaves a numbing sensation in your mouth.

CUMIN SEEDS: BROWN & BLACK

Cumin is the most versatile spice. The smell is strong, spicy and sweet, and the flavour is sharp, earthy and warm. The aroma of cumin is enhanced when the seeds are dry toasted or roasted. Black cumin seeds (*kala* or *shah jeera*) are darker and smaller than the brown seeds, and they have a very complex flavour that lies between cumin and caraway. Use sparingly.

DRIED COCKSCOMB FLOWER EXTRACT

This is indigenous to Kashmir and an important part of the *wazwan* cuisine. It adds an amazing red colour to the dishes in which it is used; for example, *rogan josh* gets its signature colour from cockscomb. In Kashmir, you can buy dried cockscomb flowers and the extract in the markets, but elsewhere you can easily source them online or from specialty stores, either whole or ground. According to author and gardening expert Jekka McVicar, they are pretty annual plants that are part of the amaranth family. To make your own cockscomb flower extract, add 6–7 dried flowers to 500 ml (17 fl oz/2 cups) boiling water. Leave to soak for 30 minutes, then strain through a muslin (cheesecloth) into a jar. It will keep for up to 2 weeks in the refrigerator. Use as directed in the recipes. (See image below, left.)

DRIED MINT

Dried mint is added to some dishes for its aromatic flavour. It has been used since ancient times.

FENNEL: GROUND & SEEDS

Ground fennel is one of the most common ingredients used in cooking sauces, pickling and curries. It has a sweet taste, which is brought out when the seeds are dry toasted and ground. When left whole, fennel seeds are warm, with an anise-liquorice aroma. They are less pungent, with a hint of camphor.

GROUND GINGER

In Kashmir and many parts of India, ground ginger is made by drying the ginger root, then grinding it into powder. In this form, it is peppery and warm, and the taste is fiery, pungent and strong.

RED KASHMIRI CHILLI

There are many different varieties of chillies, but Kashmir has deeply coloured, vibrant chillies that add colour and a delicious warmth of flavour to dishes. (See image below, right.)

SAFFRON

The world's most expensive spice, saffron needs to be soaked in warm water or milk before being added during cooking or after the dish is cooked. The saffron from Kashmir has a rich burgundy colour and the threads are long, firm and smooth. The aroma is rich, pungent and floral. The taste is delicate, warm and bitter.

TURMERIC

Ground turmeric is complex and rich, with ginger and citrus notes. The taste is slightly bitter, warm and musky.

VER MASALA (SPICE CAKE)

Ver is a traditional Kashmiri spice mix that is usually stored in small tablets or cakes, so they can easily be added to sauces. *Ver* is simple, yet very aromatic, and is usually added towards the end of cooking to enhance the flavour. According to my friend Amit there are two types of *ver masala* – the one made with asafoetida is used in Pandit cuisine, and the other one is made with garlic and *praan* (shallots) and is used in *wazwan* cooking. (See page 18 for the recipe with garlic and shallots.)

BASIC SPICES & PREPARATIONS

CHAMAN

HOMEMADE PANEER

SERVES 4

INGREDIENTS

3 LITRES (104 FL OZ/12 CUPS) FULL-FAT MILK

JUICE OF 2 LEMONS (OR 2 TEASPOONS WHITE WINE VINEGAR OR WHITE MALT VINEGAR)

Paneer is so versatile that it can be used in creamy sauces, smothered in spinach or even used to make deep-fried pakoras. During my childhood in India, my mum (who sadly passed away in 2019) would always make her own paneer for various dishes. Paneer is available in supermarkets these days, but if you're making it yourself at home, do use full-fat milk, as it gives a better result.

Pour the milk into a heavy-based saucepan and bring to the boil, then turn off the heat. Add the lemon juice or vinegar and stir. The milk will start to curdle. Stir for 5–6 minutes until the curds separate from the liquid, then remove the pan from the stove.

Line a colander with a muslin (cheesecloth) and use it to strain the curdled milk. When it has cooled down, fold up the corners of the cloth and squeeze out all the liquid you can.

Place a heavy object on the top of the cloth in the colander so all the liquid drains out. I leave it for around 2 hours to drain and firm up. To speed up the process, you can place it in the refrigerator – this helps it to firm up faster. It will keep for up to 2 days in the refrigerator. (See page 19 for the recipe photo.)

PRAAN PASTE

SHALLOT PASTE

MAKES 1 X 500 ML (1 LB 2 OZ) JAR

INGREDIENTS

125 G (4 OZ/½ CUP) GHEE

1 KG (2 LB 4 OZ) SHALLOTS, PEELED AND FINELY CHOPPED

This onion paste is used in all Kashmiri cooking, but especially in the wazwan *cuisine. It is usually made with praan shallots, but as they are difficult to find outside India, you can substitute regular echalion shallots, which have a similar strong taste. This gives a beautiful flavour when added to dishes.*

Pour the ghee into a heavy-based saucepan and heat to 170°C/340°F on a digital thermometer. Alternatively, you can drop in a tiny piece of shallot: if it floats to the surface, then the ghee is hot enough; if it sinks, the ghee is not hot enough yet.

Once the ghee is hot, add the chopped shallots in batches and fry until golden brown and crispy. Remove with a slotted spoon to a plate lined with paper towels to drain and cool.

When the crispy golden shallots have cooled down, grind to a fine paste with a pestle and mortar. You must have patience to get the right consistency. Keep grinding until the mixture changes colour to creamy white and the texture becomes like a paste. If you don't have a pestle and mortar, you can blitz in a blender, but the taste and texture won't be the same.

Store in an airtight container in the refrigerator and use in dishes when required. It will keep for up to a week.

VER MASALA

SPICE CAKE WITH GARLIC AND SHALLOTS

MAKES 10 SPICE CAKES

INGREDIENTS

100 G (3½ OZ) FRESH GARLIC, PEELED

100 G (3½ OZ) SHALLOTS, PEELED AND CHOPPED

50 ML (1¾ FL OZ/3 TABLESPOONS) RAPESEED (CANOLA) OIL

200 G (7 OZ/2 CUPS) KASHMIRI CHILLI POWDER

100 G (3½ OZ/1 CUP) GROUND GINGER

100 G (3½ OZ/1 CUP) GROUND FENNEL

15 G (½ OZ/2 TABLESPOONS) GROUND TURMERIC

10 G (½ OZ/1½ TABLESPOONS) BLACK CUMIN SEEDS

1 TABLESPOON GROUND CINNAMON

1 TEASPOON GROUND CLOVES

SEEDS OF 5 BLACK CARDAMOM PODS, CRUSHED

SEEDS OF 10 GREEN CARDAMOM PODS, CRUSHED

250 ML (8½ FL OZ/1 CUP) WATER

Ver is a traditional Kashmiri spice mix that is usually stored in small tablets or cakes, so they can easily be added to sauces. Ver is simple, yet very aromatic, and is usually added towards the end of cooking to enhance the flavour, with fennel and black cardamom being quite prominent.

Place the garlic and chopped shallots in a blender or pestle and mortar and blitz or grind to a fine paste.

Heat the oil in a small saucepan over a medium heat. Once hot, remove from the heat and let cool before adding the rest of the ingredients. Mix with gloved hands until well incorporated, kneading the mixture like a dough.

Divide into 10 balls, then flatten them. Traditionally, these would be dried in the sun until there is no moisture left, but you can place them on a baking sheet and dehydrate them in a low oven for 2 hours. Store in an airtight container to use when needed. It will keep for up to a month. When using in the dishes, add about 1–2 teaspoons, or as directed in the recipe.

DAHI

HOMEMADE YOGHURT

SERVES 4

INGREDIENTS

600 ML (20 FL OZ/2½ CUPS) FULL-FAT (WHOLE) MILK

3 TEASPOONS CULTURED (LIVE/PROBIOTIC) YOGHURT

When I was growing up, yoghurt was always made at home and never store-bought. As there are so many recipes that include yoghurt in this book, I wanted to share the recipe for making your own yoghurt at home.

Pour the milk into a saucepan and bring to the boil, then remove from the heat and let it cool to room temperature.

Pour the cooled milk into a suitable container – I recommend a baked clay dish, but you can also use a casserole dish with a lid. Mix the yoghurt into the milk, then cover with the lid and wrap in a blanket. Leave overnight at room temperature and it will be set in the morning.

Store in the refrigerator for 2–3 days.

ER MASALA   PAGE 18

HOMEMADE PANEER   PAGE 17

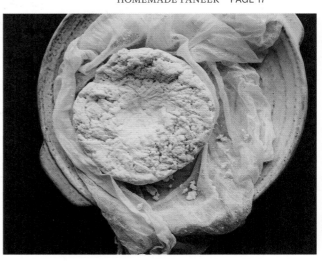

KASHMIRI SAFFRON – A TALE OF AN EXPENSIVE SPICE

THE LEGEND OF KASHMIRI SAFFRON

Throughout India, saffron has many names: *kong posh* in Kashmiri, *kesar* in Hindi, *zafran* in Urdu, among others. As well as numerous names, there are various stories of how it ended up being such an integral part of Kashmiri agriculture and cuisine.

Some claim that the spice was brought to the region by two Sufi saints: Khwaja Masood Wali and Sheikl Sharif-u-din. When both saints fell ill on their travels to Kashmir, a local chieftain cured them of their illness. In return, they presented him with the gift of a saffron bulb.

Others believe that Persians introduced saffron to Kashmir, selling it to locals as they passed through. The famous Kashmiri poet Mohammed Yusuf Teng disagreed, claiming that Kashmir had cultivated the plant for more than two millennia.

Later, it was the Mughals – the Central Asian Turkic kings – who began to inhabit India in the 16th century, who brought saffron into the royal kitchens. Here, it became popular not only in dishes – but was also used in flatbreads, stews and sweet dishes.

These disagreements over the history of Kashmir's love affair with saffron add a sense of mystery and intrigue: perfect for this incredible spice, with its unique taste and aroma, and a hint of bitterness.

JUST A FEW WEEKS OF BEAUTIFUL BLOOMS

The saffron crocus flowers bloom for just two weeks of every year. From the middle of October to the beginning of November, families harvest the saffron. Pampore in the Pulwama district is renowned for growing the very best quality saffron, so I was desperate to meet the growers and learn more about this treasured, vivid crimson spice.

As I passed through the tin-roofed shops of Pampore, my driver told me that for the majority of the year the surrounding landscapes are unexceptional. It's only during harvest season that the land fills with colour, with rolling fields of light purple saffron blooms as far as the eye can see. I had never seen saffron fields before, so I was excited, not only to travel to see Pampore, but also to meet the families, growers and sellers, and visit the town's trade centre to understand the importance of this magical spice to the region, and why the government's help is so vital.

En route to my first destination, I met a saffron grower and shop owner. I stopped for *kahwa* – a traditional Kashmiri green tea steeped with cinnamon, cardamom and saffron – outside his shop. It was the best I tasted in my time in Kashmir. I felt lucky to have experienced the end product in its homeland. Next, I travelled to the Indian International Kashmir Saffron Trading Centre (IIKSTC) – a building that remarkably few know exists. Here, the government works to restore the pristine glory of Kashmiri saffron cultivation and trade.

The building is a maze of rooms, throughout which different parts of the saffron preparation process are conducted. I had no idea how much work went into producing the spice. From plucking the saffron strands to weighing and drying, I learned a great deal about the meticulous work that goes into creating these highly prized crimson strands. There are no seeds in the flower, just red stigma and yellow stamens, and each plant produces just one crop a year. Sadly, the crop has dropped in production in Kashmir were last year's yield being the lowest ever – a fact that the farmers I spoke to were incredibly emotional about.

I met farmer Abdul Majid Wani, who described how, at harvest time, he would head out into the fields with his family and the whole area would be filled with the sounds of happy laughter. Now, he says, the plucking and separating processes are extremely fast and mechanised, and things just aren't the same.

THE FUTURE OF KASHMIRI SAFFRON

I met with Dr Inam-ur Rasool and Tariq Parrey of the IIKSTC, who told me how the facility is working with the Department of Agriculture to promote GI-tagged Kashmiri saffron. This certifies that the product genuinely does hail from the region. They are also formulating plans for e-auctioning, which will allow growers to get the best returns for their product to boost the local economy, and to reassure buyers that the saffron they buy through the platform will be tested and certified high quality Kashmiri produce.

The introduction of GI tagging and e-auctions has created a lot of positive emotion in Kashmiri people, but these changes are necessary if the cultivation and trading of the spice is to survive. Saffron farmers are facing ecological struggles, with climate change causing droughts that can make growing conditions near impossible, and a land that was once prosperous is diminishing in its returns. As a result, many farmers and villagers have begun to abandon their land – and this has been hastened by the introduction of the Armed Force Special Power Act, granted to the military in 1990, which allows the armed forces to search and arrest individuals, leading to huge mistrust of the government.

It is a situation I have pondered deeply. I firmly believe that the older generation of saffron farmers are in need to motivation and support, and that the industry needs the involvement of the younger generations in order to survive. Despite all their struggles and the violence they've faced, many families are still associated with the Kashmiri saffron economy today, which is heartening to know. But with so many changes to the industry – and rumours that lower-priced Iranian saffron has begun to enter India and is being packaged and sold as Kashmiri saffron – what does the future hold for this evocative spice in the region?

NASHTA

SNACKS & STARTERS

Nashta is the first meal of the day, but in many states of India, we have it in the evening too.

Snacks come in a variety of forms in Kashmir. Traditionally, they are prepared from ingredients available at home, unless they are being made for a special occasion (they make great appetisers if you are entertaining guests). The recipes in this section are the ones I ate during my time in Kashmir, but there are many more to be discovered.

Every state has its own type of snacks, and it's so fascinating to learn more about the different styles of cooking. It's all about food, cultures and community – and simple flavours done well.

WANGUN PAKORE

AUBERGINE PAKORAS

SERVES 4 (MAKES 24)

Pakoras are a spiced fritter, made at home, and sold by street vendors all over India. While in Jammu and Kashmir, I tasted pakoras made with rice-flour and gram-flour batters. Rice-flour pakoras stay crispy longer then the gram-flour ones, but both types are crispy and delicious when served hot. Enjoy with tomato ketchup.

In a large bowl, sift together the flour, chilli powder and salt. Slowly add the water, whisking it until you get a batter of the consistency you would use for pancakes. Add the aubergine slices to the batter and stir to coat.

Pour sunflower oil into a deep, heavy-based pan to a depth of 8 cm (3 in). Place over a medium heat and heat to 180°C/350°F on a digital thermometer. Alternatively, you can drop in a tiny piece of bread or batter: if it sizzles and browns in 15 seconds, the oil is hot enough.

Once the oil is hot, carefully lower the batter-coated aubergine slices into the oil and deep-fry for 4–5 minutes until crispy and brown. Remove with a slotted spoon to drain on a plate lined with paper towels. You may need to do these in batches of about 5 at a time so they remain separate and the oil temperature stays high enough.

Serve hot immediately, otherwise they lose their crispiness. If you have leftovers and want to eat them later, reheat them in the oven rather than in a microwave.

INGREDIENTS

200 G (7 OZ/1⅔ CUPS) CHICKPEA (GRAM) FLOUR

2 TEASPOONS KASHMIRI CHILLI POWDER

1 TEASPOON SALT

75–100 ML (2½–3½ FL OZ/5 TABLESPOONS–SCANT ½ CUP) WATER

6 AUBERGINES (EGGPLANTS), STALK REMOVED, CUT LENGTHWAYS INTO THIN SLICES

SUNFLOWER OIL, FOR DEEP-FRYING

AAL POSH MOND

FRIED PUMPKIN OR COURGETTE
FLOWERS

SERVES 4

*This recipe takes me back to when my grandma would pick
pumpkin flowers on our summer holidays to Punjab. She
would prepare them in a Punjabi way: making a batter
with gram flour, green chillies and a variety of spices
before frying.*

*In Jammu and Kashmir, I had the experience of seeing
them prepared in a different way, coated in a rice flour
batter with red Kashmiri chilli, turmeric and fennel. Here,
I've given the option of using courgette (zucchini) flowers
instead of pumpkin (squash) flowers, as they are easier to
find outside of India.*

In a large bowl, sift together the rice flour, spices and salt.
Slowly add the water, whisking it until you get a pancake
batter consistency. Gently place the pumpkin or courgette
flowers in the batter, turning them to coat.

Meanwhile, pour sunflower oil into a deep, heavy-
based pan to a depth of 8 cm (3 in). Place over a medium
heat and heat to 180°C/350°F on a digital thermometer.
Alternatively, you can drop in a tiny piece of bread: if it
sizzles and browns in 15 seconds, the oil is hot enough.

Once the oil is hot, carefully lower the batter-coated
flowers into the oil and deep-fry for 4–5 minutes until
crispy and brown. Remove with a slotted spoon to
drain on a plate lined with paper towels. You may need
to do these in batches of about 6 at a time so the oil
temperature remains high enough.

Serve hot, sprinkled with sea salt, some lime wedges
and a chutney of your choice.

INGREDIENTS

150 G (5 OZ/SCANT 1 CUP) RICE FLOUR

2 TEASPOONS KASHMIRI CHILLI POWDER

1 TEASPOON GROUND TURMERIC

1 TEASPOON GROUND FENNEL

1 TEASPOON GROUND GINGER

1 TEASPOON SALT

200 ML (7 FL OZ/SCANT 1 CUP) WATER

12 PUMPKIN (SQUASH) OR COURGETTE
(ZUCCHINI) FLOWERS

SUNFLOWER OIL, FOR DEEP-FRYING

TO SERVE

SEA SALT, TO SPRINKLE

LIME WEDGES

CHUTNEY OF YOUR CHOICE (OPTIONAL)

SEE IMAGE   PAGES 30–31 →

NADIR MONJ

FRIED LOTUS ROOT

SERVES 4–6

Lotus root is used a lot in Kashmiri cuisine. I love these delicious delicacies, which are often served as street food. On a visit to the Hazratbal Shrine, I brought some of these back to the hotel I was staying in, to have with a cup of tea. This recipe was kindly given to me by the sweet food vendor when I asked him which ingredients he used for the batter mix. Lotus root is readily available in Chinese and other Asian grocers – you can also find them ready sliced in the frozen section in the supermarket. I am not a big fan of the canned ones.

In a large bowl, mix together the flour, chilli powder, ground ginger and salt, then add the water and mix to a smooth, fine paste. Add the lotus root slices, turning to coat them in the paste.

Meanwhile, pour sunflower oil into a deep, heavy-based pan to a depth of 8 cm (3 in). Place over a medium heat and heat to 180°C/350°F on a digital thermometer. Alternatively, you can drop in a tiny piece of bread or batter: if it sizzles and browns in 15 seconds, the oil is hot enough.

Once the oil is hot, carefully lower the lotus root slices into the oil and deep-fry until brown and crispy. Remove with a slotted spoon to drain on a plate lined with paper towels. You may need to do these in batches of about 6 at a time so the oil temperature remains high enough.

Serve hot. I love to eat them with chutney or even tomato ketchup.

INGREDIENTS

75 G (2½ OZ/SCANT ⅔ CUP) RICE FLOUR

1–2 TEASPOONS KASHMIRI CHILLI POWDER

1 TEASPOON GROUND GINGER

1 TEASPOON SALT

200 ML (7 FL OZ/SCANT 1 CUP) WATER

500 G (1 LB 2 OZ) LOTUS ROOT, WASHED, PEELED, AND CUT INTO THIN STRIPS

SUNFLOWER OIL, FOR DEEP-FRYING

ANY CHUTNEY OR TOMATO KETCHUP, TO SERVE

LEFT AND BOTTOM

A sweet food vendor on a street
inside the city.

SHEEKH KEBAB

SKEWERED LAMB KEBABS

SERVES 3–4

While in Srinagar, I ate sheekh kebab *at a few places – it is a popular appetiser and I am a huge fan. This recipe has perfect balance of flavours and is super easy to make at home.*

Combine all the ingredients, except the egg, in a large mixing bowl. Mix together, kneading as you would a dough, until well combined. Cover and refrigerate for 1 hour.

Remove from the refrigerator, then place the mixture in a food processor. Add the egg and blend to a paste.

Divide the mixture into 6 equal-sized portions. Wet your hands with cold water and mould each portion around a skewer, gently pressing and shaping each into a long sausage. With damp hands, smooth the surface of each kebab.

Meanwhile, prepare a barbecue or preheat the oven grill (broiler) to high.

Cook the skewers on the hot barbecue or under the grill for 8–10 minutes, turning them after 5 minutes and rotating them frequently until well browned and cooked on all sides.

Serve scattered with coriander and sliced shallots, with lime wedges for squeezing and a chutney of your choice, if you like.

INGREDIENTS

1 KG (2 LB 4 OZ) MINCED (GROUND) LAMB (IDEALLY LEG MEAT)

2–3 TEASPOONS KASHMIRI CHILLI POWDER

1½ TEASPOONS SALT

1 TEASPOON DRIED MINT

1 TSP GROUND CUMIN

1 TEASPOON SAFFRON STRANDS

1 TSP BLACK CARDAMOM SEEDS, CRUSHED TO A POWDER IN A PESTLE AND MORTAR

½ TEASPOON BLACK CUMIN SEEDS, CRUSHED TO A POWDER IN A PESTLE AND MORTAR

HANDFUL OF FRESH CORIANDER (CILANTRO) LEAVES, CHOPPED, PLUS EXTRA TO SERVE

1 LARGE EGG, LIGHTLY BEATEN

TO SERVE

SLICED SHALLOTS

LIME WEDGES

CHUTNEY OF YOUR CHOICE (OPTIONAL)

SHAMMI KEBAB

MINCED LAMB PATTIES

MAKES 12

There are so many different kebabs made all over India. These shammi kebabs *remind me of my trip to Lucknow. I still remember how huge the queue was for the kebabs. My daughters loves these too, because they are soft and moist. I always add gram flour to make sure the patties bind. Some people don't bother with it, but I think it helps them to hold together well.*

Put all the ingredients, except the fresh coriander, flour and oil, in a large saucepan. Bring to the boil, then reduce the heat and cook for 30 minutes until the *chana dal* is cooked and the water has reduced. If there is still a little water left, strain the mixture to eradicate any excess liquid. Leave to cool.

Discard the whole spices and transfer the mixture to a food processor along with the fresh coriander. Blitz to a rough paste. Don't turn it into a purée, as it won't hold together properly. Add the flour, if using, and blitz to combine. Transfer to a bowl and refrigerate for about 30 minutes.

Divide the mixture into 12 equal-sized portions and shape each one into a patty.

You can either shallow-fry or deep-fry the patties. For deep frying, pour the oil into a deep, heavy-based pan so that it is half full. Set the pan over medium heat. If you have a digital thermometer, then heat the oil to 175°C/ 347°F. Alternatively, drop a tiny bit of the kebab mixture into the oil, to test if it is ready. If the mixture floats up, the oil is hot enough. To shallow fry, you just need to heat enough oil in a frying pan (skillet) until it is hot. Test the heat of the oil with a small piece of kebab mixture before you start to fry the patties.

Fry the patties for 3–4 minutes on each side until golden brown and cooked through. You many need to do this in batches depending on the size of your pan.

Serve with raw sliced onions or a raita of your choice, and with lime or lemon wedges on the side for squeezing.

INGREDIENTS

500 G (1 LB 2 OZ) GOOD-QUALITY MINCED (GROUND) LAMB (OR GOAT)

100 G (3½ OZ/½ CUP) CHANA DAL (SPLIT CHICKPEAS)

6 GARLIC CLOVES, PEELED

8 CM (3 IN) CINNAMON STICK

5 BLACK CARDAMOM PODS

6 GREEN CARDAMOM PODS

2 TEASPOONS KASHMIRI CHILLI POWDER

2 TEASPOONS GROUND GINGER

1 TEASPOON GROUND TURMERIC

1 TEASPOON GROUND FENNEL

1 TEASPOON SALT

800 ML (27 FL OZ/GENEROUS 3 CUPS) WATER

HANDFUL OF FRESH CORIANDER (CILANTRO), LEAVES AND STEMS, ROUGHLY CHOPPED

50 G (2 OZ/½ CUP) CHICKPEA (GRAM) FLOUR (OPTIONAL)

SUNFLOWER OIL, FOR SHALLOW- OR DEEP-FRYING

TO SERVE

SLICED ONIONS OR CUCUMBER OR RADISH RAITA (PAGE 196)

LIME OR LEMON WEDGES

KOKUR MASALA

CHICKEN MASALA

SERVES 4

While I was in Kashmir, I didn't have any chicken dishes in the restaurants, only in the homes I was invited to, but the flavours I got to taste there were utterly delicious. This combination of shallots and chicken is perfect. You can eat this as a starter or as a main meal with rice or salad.

Place the chicken drumsticks in a large bowl. Add ½ teaspoon of the salt and 1 teaspoon of the chilli powder, and mix together.

Pour sunflower oil into a deep, heavy-based pan to a depth of 8 cm (3 in). Place over a medium heat and heat to 180°C/350°F on a digital thermometer. Alternatively, you can drop in a tiny piece of bread: if it sizzles and browns in 15 seconds, the oil is hot enough.

Once the oil is hot, add the chicken drumsticks and fry for 10–12 minutes until brown and crispy all over. You may need to do this in batches. Set them aside on a plate.

Heat 5 teaspoons of oil in a separate frying pan (skillet) over a medium heat. Add the bay leaves and cinnamon stick, then add the sliced shallots and cook for 10–15 minutes until dark brown. Add all the spices, including the remaining ½ teaspoon salt and 1 teaspoon chilli powder, then pour in the water. Cook, stirring, for 1 minute, then add the fried chicken and cook, still over a medium heat, for 20 minutes.

Serve hot, garnished with coriander and chopped green chillies.

INGREDIENTS

8 CHICKEN DRUMSTICKS (REMOVE THE SKIN)

1 TEASPOON SALT

2 TEASPOONS KASHMIRI CHILLI POWDER

SUNFLOWER OIL, FOR FRYING

3 DRIED BAY LEAVES

8 CM (3 IN) CINNAMON STICK

400 G (14 OZ) SHALLOTS, THINLY SLICED

2 TEASPOONS GROUND CUMIN

1 TEASPOON GROUND GINGER

1 TEASPOON GROUND TURMERIC

3 BLACK CARDAMOM PODS, SEEDS CRUSHED AND GROUND INTO A POWDER IN A PESTLE AND MORTAR

SEEDS FROM 5 GREEN CARDAMOM PODS, GROUND INTO A POWDER IN A PESTLE AND MORTAR

100 ML (3½ FL OZ/SCANT ½ CUP) WATER

FRESH CORIANDER (CILANTRO) LEAVES, TO GARNISH

2 GREEN CHILLES, ROUGHLY CHOPPED, TO GARNISH

MULAQAT –
A MEETING WITH AMIT

I was in Srinagar on my second visit to Kashmir when I met Amit, a man who my chef friend, Thomas, had introduced me to. Formerly a doctor, Amit left medicine and now runs a communications agency, and Thomas knew he had connections and knowledge that would serve me well in getting to know the region, its people, its food and its culture.

The only contact I'd had with Amit had been via WhatsApp – we had never met in person. On the trip I made for this book, I finally got to opportunity to visit his house for lunch and meet him and his family for the first time. Before I knew it, I was showered with a proper Kashmiri Pandit vegetarian feast: hearty *dum aloo* (baby potatoes in a thick, yoghurt-based gravy with plenty of fennel), *Kashmiri haakh* (simple greens, which retain a little bite and feature just a hint of chilli), *katte baigan* (a tamarind-infused aubergine dish), and *paneer kyalia* (curd cheese with aromatic spices, *nadru yakhni* (lotus stems in an aromatic yoghurt gravy) rounded off the meal, all served with mooli chutney and rice. I was in a very happy, contented place. Amit's mother reminded me of my own mum, who was just as passionate about cooking for and feeding other people.

Throughout the meal, I chatted with Amit about Kashmir's food, people and beauty – and what sticks most in my mind is a story he told me about his family's history. He talked about his grandfather, social activist Hridai Nath Wanchoo, who was known as the most important human rights activist in Kashmir, and worked tirelessly to improve workers' rights, healthcare provision and more. On December 5, 1992, the day before activists attacked and demolished the Babri Masjid mosque in Ayodhya, Wanchoo was assassinated – shot dead by three unidentified gunmen in Balgarden, Srinagar. In the three days following his death, Kashmir all but closed down as people gathered to pay their respects. Even after what happened to Amit's family, they stood their ground and remained in Kashmir, unlike many others who fled the region in the 1990s.

After our glorious – and thought-provoking – lunch, Amit took us to meet a team of *wazas*, who were cooking for a party. Preparation for a *wazwan* is time-consuming and labour-intensive, and care must be taken to get everything just right. Each *waza* had their own part to play in creating the feast, much like a group of musicians coming together to play a piece of orchestral music. I was overwhelmed by the sights, sounds and smells of all of the big pots cooking. It all whetted my appetite, despite the fact I had just eaten – and, of course, I sampled most of the dishes.

As we all know, no matter how full we are after a big meal, there is always space for something sweet! It is just as well, as the rest of my day was spent on a tour of Srinagar's bakeries, beginning with the Jee Enn bakery – one of the oldest in the city, having opened in the 1970s. While they are famous for many things, it was their coconut macaroons and eclairs that won my heart. From there, we moved on to the Moonlight bakery and sampled their renowned walnut fudge: a delectable mixture of honey, walnuts and dates.

As the sun began to set, before I travelled back towards my hotel, I took the *shikara* (boatride), the lapping of the water and the swish of the oars giving me a sense of calm amongst the hustle and bustle of tourists enjoying the sunset views. My final visit of the day, before returning to the hotel, was to the Mughal Darbar Bakery and Restaurant, which has been in the same home on Residency Road since 1982. Founder Haji Mohammad Ibrahim Mugloo wanted to bring *wazwan* to people from all walks of life, and although he passed away in 2018 it remains a family business thanks to the efforts of his sons. Despite my fatigue, I enjoyed a hearty meal of traditional delicacies, and at the end bought a fruit cake for us to share in the morning, knowing that we would have an early start: one of the many benefits of the fact that so many Kashmiri restaurants have a bakery attached.

SEYUN

VEGETARIAN

Vegetarian dishes played a huge part in my upbringing. In this chapter, I wanted to share some of the vegetable-based recipes I enjoyed throughout Kashmir. *Seyun* are vegetable dishes cooked with simple spices to create warming meals that taste incredible.

Due to the harsh climate, most of the vegetables are dried in summer to preserve them throughout the year. The beauty of these recipes is that each is slightly different, and they can be enjoyed by everyone.

HAAKH

KASHMIRI SPINACH

SERVES 3

Haakh *is eaten by many Kashmiris as a main dish, served simply with rice or flatbreads. However, others will eat it as a side dish alongside meat.*

This recipe is so simple, yet so delicious. The first time I tasted it, I had to go back for seconds. The greens used in Kashmir are different to the varieties found elsewhere, so your greens might take less water and less time to cook. I would recommend using long spinach leaves rather than baby spinach.

Heat the oil in a deep, heavy-based pan over a medium heat. Add the chillies and asafoetida and cook for 1 minute, then add the spinach, salt, turmeric and water, and mix well. Bring to the boil, then cover the pan with a lid and cook over a medium heat for about 4–5 minutes until the spinach is tender and very little water remains.

Serve in a bowl with the remaining cooking liquid.

INGREDIENTS

40 ML (SCANT 3 TABLESPOONS) MUSTARD OIL

4 DRIED WHOLE RED KASHMIRI CHILLIES

½ TEASPOON ASAFOETIDA POWDER

750 G (1 LB 10 OZ) SPINACH, WASHED

1 TEASPOON SALT

1 TEASPOON TURMERIC

250 ML (8½ FL OZ/1 CUP) WATER

HAAKH TE NADIR

SPINACH WITH LOTUS ROOT

SERVES 3–4

Spinach is one of those leafy vegetables that catches other flavours well. I had never had spinach cooked with lotus root before, but I tried this in a hotel restaurant in Kashmir and I found the combination to be a perfect harmony. Paneer is very popular in other parts of India, and it can be used instead of lotus stem in this recipe.

If using fresh lotus root, place the pieces in a saucepan, cover with boiling water and cook for 15–20 minutes until tender. Drain and set aside.

In a separate pan, cover the spinach with the 200 ml (7 fl oz/scant 1 cup) water. Bring to the boil and cook for 4–5 minutes, then remove from the heat and leave to cool. Do not drain; instead, mash and set aside.

Heat the oil in a frying pan over a medium heat. When the oil is hot, add the asafoetida, dried chillies, turmeric, ginger and salt. Add the cooked lotus root (or canned, if using) and cook for 3–4 minutes, then add the mashed greens, along with their cooking water. Bring to the boil, then reduce the heat to low. Cover with a lid and cook for a further 15 minutes.

Serve with rice.

INGREDIENTS

200 G (7 OZ) FRESH LOTUS ROOT, PEELED AND CUT INTO THIN ROUNDS (YOU COULD USE CANNED, DRAINED LOTUS ROOT, IF NEEDED)

500 G (1 LB 2 OZ) SPINACH

200 ML (7 FL OZ/SCANT 1 CUP) WATER

5 TEASPOONS RAPESEED (CANOLA) OIL

½ TEASPOON ASAFOETIDA POWDER

3 DRIED WHOLE KASHMIRI CHILLIES

1 TEASPOON GROUND TURMERIC

1 TEASPOON GROUND GINGER

1 TEASPOON SALT

STEAMED RICE, TO SERVE

CHAMAN KALIYA

PANEER IN YELLOW GRAVY

SERVES 4

When I was travelling in Kashmir, many restaurants, hotels and home cooks were using paneer and cooking it in ways I wasn't used to. This particular recipe was inspired by my friends Amit and Prateek's parents, whom I met when they were visiting Kashmir. I had never eaten paneer this way before.

This beautiful, tasty bowl of yellow sunshine is so good that you will be going back for seconds. A simple yet delectable dish.

Heat the oil in a large pan over a medium heat. Add the paneer and fry until light brown on all sides. Remove from the pan and set aside.

Add all the whole spices and bay leaves to the pan and cook for 1 minute, then add the asafoetida, turmeric, ginger, fennel, salt and halved chillies. Cook, stirring, for 1 minute, then pour in the hot water. Increase the heat and bring to the boil. Now reduce the heat back to medium, add the fried paneer and cook for 3 minutes. Pour in the milk and cook for a further 5–6 minutes until the gravy thickens. Mix through the dried fenugreek leaves and remove from the heat.

Serve with rice.

INGREDIENTS

3 TABLESPOONS MUSTARD OIL

500 G (1 LB 2 OZ) PANEER, CUT INTO CUBES

8 GREEN CARDAMOM PODS

4 BLACK CARDAMOM PODS

4 CLOVES

1 TEASPOON BROWN CUMIN SEEDS

2-3 DRIED BAY LEAVES

½ TEASPOON ASAFOETIDA POWDER

1 TEASPOON GROUND TURMERIC

1 TEASPOON GROUND GINGER

1½ TEASPOON GROUND FENNEL

1 TEASPOON SALT

2 WHOLE GREEN CHILLIES, HALVED LENGTHWAYS

300 ML (10 FL OZ/1¼ CUPS) HOT WATER

300 ML (10 FL OZ/1¼ CUPS) FULL-FAT (WHOLE) MILK

1 TEASPOON DRIED FENUGREEK LEAVES (KASURI METHI)

STEAMED RICE, TO SERVE

RUANGAN CHAMAN

PANEER IN TOMATO GRAVY

SERVES 4

Kashmiri ruangan chaman *is a delicate, tangy and exquisite dish. Chaman* means paneer in Kashmiri. *When I came back home and started testing recipes, this became my husband's favourite dish. Some cooks I met preferred to blanch and peel the tomatoes before puréeing them, but you don't have to do this. Serve with rice or flatbreads.*

Place the tomatoes in a food processor and blend to a purée. Set aside.

Heat the ghee or oil in a frying pan (skillet) over a medium heat. Add the paneer and fry until light brown on all sides. Remove and set aside.

Add the cinnamon stick to the pan, along with the tomato purée, and cook for 3–4 minutes. Add the Kashmiri chilli paste, turmeric, ginger, crushed cardamom seeds and salt, and cook for 2 minutes. Add the hot water and increase the heat to bring to the boil, then reduce the heat back to medium, cover and cook for 5–6 minutes until the gravy is thick.

Remove the lid and stir through the fried paneer, dried mint or methi, black cumin seeds and cockscomb extract (if using). Cook for a further 5 minutes.

Leave to rest for at least 30 minutes before serving with rice or flatbreads.

INGREDIENTS

300 G (10½ OZ) TOMATOES, CUT INTO CHUNKS

4 TEASPOONS GHEE OR 2 TABLESPOONS MUSTARD OIL

400 G (14 OZ) PANEER, SLICED INTO STRIPS

8 CM (3 IN) CINNAMON STICK

1–2 TEASPOONS KASHMIRI CHILLI PASTE

1 TEASPOON GROUND TURMERIC

1 TEASPOON GROUND GINGER

1 TEASPOON CRUSHED GREEN CARDAMOM SEEDS

1 TEASPOON SALT

400 ML (13 FL OZ/GENEROUS 1½ CUPS) HOT WATER

1 TEASPOON DRIED MINT OR DRIED FENUGREEK LEAVES (KASURI METHI)

½ TEASPOON BLACK CUMIN SEEDS

70 ML (2½ FL OZ/5 TABLESPOONS) COCKSCOMB FLOWER EXTRACT (PAGES 15–16) (OPTIONAL)

STEAMED RICE OR FLATBREADS, TO SERVE

MONJ HAAKH

KASHMIRI KOHLRABI

SERVES 3–4

The kohlrabi I've eaten in the UK has mostly been in the form of salads, but what really made me fall in love with the food in Kashmir was the simplicity of the spices and cooking methods used to transform such humble ingredients. In this recipe, I combine spices with fresh kohlrabi, but in Kashmir, they tend to dry the kohlrabi so it can also be used during the winter months, when the weather is harsh and fewer vegetables grow.

Remove and wash the kohlrabi leaves, then remove and discard the stems. Place the leaves in a saucepan and pour over 100 ml (3½ fl oz/scant ½ cup) boiling water. Blanch for 2–3 minutes. Drain, reserving the cooking water, and roughly chop. Set aside.

Peel the kohlrabi bulb, and cut into slices or 2 cm (¾ in) chunks.

Heat the ghee in a large pan over a medium heat, add the kohlrabi slices/chunks and cook for 10–12 minutes, stirring occasionally. Add the chopped leaves, dried chillies, turmeric, salt and asafoetida, along with the reserved kohlrabi cooking water. Top up with another 200 ml (7 fl oz/scant 1 cup) water. Mix well and cook for a further 5 minutes.

Spoon into bowls and serve with rice or flatbreads.

INGREDIENTS

500 G (1 LB 2 OZ) KOHLRABI WITH LEAVES

3 HEAPED TEASPOONS GHEE

3 DRIED WHOLE RED KASHMIRI CHILLIES

1 TEASPOON GROUND TURMERIC

1 TEASPOON SALT

½ TEASPOON ASAFOETIDA POWDER

STEAMED RICE OR FLATBREADS, TO SERVE

DUM OLUV

WHOLE POTATOES IN SPICY RED GRAVY

SERVES 3–4

Potatoes are used widely in Indian cuisine. Dum aloo *or* dum oluv *is cooked in a variety of ways in different regions – this version is a must try. To get the fiery, beautiful, deep red colour, you need to use the right chillies – Kashmiri chillies. Deep-frying the cooked potatoes is a very important step in this beautiful dish. Amit told me that many people also add turmeric to this recipe, and that not many people add the cockscomb extract these days.*

Boil the potatoes for 15–30 minutes until tender. Drain and plunge into iced water for a couple of minutes. Peel away the skins (they should come away easily) and carefully prick the potatoes with a toothpick or fork.

Heat the oil in a wok or deep, heavy-based pan over a medium-high heat until very hot. Add the potatoes and deep-fry until golden brown. Remove from the pan with a slotted spoon and set aside to drain on a plate lined with paper towels.

Add the bay leaves, cinnamon stick, cloves, cardamom pods, ground spices, crushed garlic and salt to the same pan. Carefully add the water and bring to the boil, then reduce the heat to low and add the whisked yoghurt. Keep stirring so the mixture doesn't split.

Return the fried potatoes to the pan and bring the mixture to the boil over a medium heat. Simmer for 10 minutes, then add the cockscomb flower extract (if using) and cook for a further 3–4 minutes. Remove from the heat and mix in the black cumin seeds.

Serve hot, with rice or flatbreads.

INGREDIENTS

500 G (1 LB 2 OZ) SMALL WAXY POTATOES (JERSEY ROYALS OR SIMILAR)

120 ML (4 FL OZ/½ CUP) SUNFLOWER OIL

3 BAY LEAVES

8 CM (3 IN) CINNAMON STICK

2 WHOLE CLOVES

4 GREEN CARDAMOM PODS

4 BLACK CARDAMOM PODS

1 TEASPOON GROUND FENNEL

1 TEASPOON GROUND GINGER

2 TEASPOONS KASHMIRI CHILLI POWDER

4 GARLIC CLOVES, CRUSHED TO A PASTE

1 TEASPOON SALT

400 ML (13 FL OZ/GENEROUS 1½ CUPS) WATER

75 G (2½ OZ/SCANT ⅓ CUP) GREEK YOGHURT, WHISKED

100 ML (3½ FL OZ/SCANT ½ CUP) COCKSCOMB FLOWER EXTRACT (PAGES 15–16) (OPTIONAL)

½ TEASPOON BLACK CUMIN SEEDS

STEAMED RICE OR FLATBREADS, TO SERVE

RAZMAH

RED KIDNEY BEANS

SERVES 5–6

When I went to Jammu about five years ago, I had this dish cooked for me by family friends who'd moved there from Kashmir in the early 1990s. In India, we mostly use dried kidney beans, soaking them overnight and then cooking them in a pressure cooker until soft. However, I have used canned beans here, for ease and speed. This is a great dish to make for a busy weeknight meal, as it can be prepared so quickly. Simply serve with cooked rice.

Heat the ghee in a large pan over a medium heat. Add the whole spices and bay leaves, and fry for 1 minute. Add the ground ginger, fennel, turmeric, chilli powder and salt. Stir together then add the kidney beans and cook over a high heat for a couple of minutes. Add the hot water and bring to the boil, then reduce the heat, cover and cook for 15 minutes, stirring occasionally.

Remove from the heat and leave to rest for 30 minutes before serving with rice. While resting, the beans soak up the beautiful juices and the dish becomes more flavourful.

INGREDIENTS

1 TABLESPOON GHEE

6 GREEN CARDAMOM PODS

4 BLACK CARDAMOM PODS

8 CM (3 IN) CINNAMON STICK

3 DRIED BAY LEAVES

2 TEASPOONS GROUND GINGER

1 TEASPOON GROUND FENNEL

1 TEASPOON GROUND TURMERIC

2 TEASPOONS KASHMIRI CHILLI POWDER

1 TEASPOON SALT

600 G (1 LB 5 OZ) CANNED KIDNEY BEANS, DRAINED AND RINSED (OR 250 G/9 OZ/ GENEROUS 1½ CUPS DRIED KIDNEY BEANS, SOAKED OVERNIGHT, THEN DRAINED AND COOKED UNTIL TENDER)

1 LITRE (34 FL OZ/4 CUPS) HOT WATER

STEAMED RICE, TO SERVE

NADIR YAKHNI

LOTUS ROOT IN YOGHURT GRAVY

SERVES 4

Yoghurt and lotus root are commonly used ingredients in Kashmiri cuisine. The creamy yoghurt pairs so well with lotus root, as the subtle balance of sourness works perfectly. You can also drizzle over some melted ghee and dried mint for an extra garnish, if you wish.

Place the lotus root in a saucepan with the measured hot water and boil for 30 minutes until half cooked. Drain and set aside.

Meanwhile, heat the ghee or oil in a separate pan with a lid over a medium heat. Add the bay leaves, cinnamon stick and cardamom pods and cook for 1 minute, then reduce the heat to low. Add the ground fennel and ginger, whisked yoghurt mixture and salt, and cook for 5–6 minutes. Add the half-cooked lotus root, cover and cook for 15–20 minutes, until tender.

Mix in the dried mint, black cumin seeds and crushed cloves before serving with rice.

INGREDIENTS

400 G (14 OZ) LOTUS ROOT, SCRAPED, WASHED AND CUT INTO 1 CM (½ IN) SLICES (YOU COULD USE CANNED, DRAINED LOTUS ROOT, IF NEEDED)

1 LITRE (34 FL OZ/4 CUPS) HOT WATER

4 TEASPOONS GHEE OR RAPESEED (CANOLA) OIL

2 DRIED BAY LEAVES

8 CM (3 IN) CINNAMON STICK

2 BLACK CARDAMOM PODS

4 GREEN CARDAMOM PODS

1½ TEASPOONS GROUND FENNEL

1 TEASPOON GROUND GINGER

300 G (10½ OZ/1¼ CUPS) GREEK YOGHURT, WHISKED WITH 300 ML (10½ FL OZ/1¼ CUPS) WATER

1 TEASPOON SALT

½ TEASPOON DRIED MINT

1 TEASPOON BLACK CUMIN SEEDS

4 WHOLE CLOVES, CRUSHED

STEAMED RICE, TO SERVE

HAEMBE TE NADIR

FRENCH BEANS WITH LOTUS ROOT

SERVES 4

French beans on their own are delicious, but adding lotus root takes them to another level. It is important to Kashmiris to make use of local, sustainable ingredients. With their harsh climate, they must use what is available.

Place the lotus root in a saucepan, cover with water and cook for 15–20 minutes until soft. Drain and set aside.

Heat the oil in a frying pan (skillet) over a medium heat. Add the ver masala, cooked lotus root and French beans and cook for 3–4 minutes. Add the salt, chilli paste and ground ginger and mix well, then add the measured hot water. Mix again, then cover and cook for 10 minutes until the vegetables are soft.

Serve with rice or flatbreads.

INGREDIENTS

250 G (9 OZ) LOTUS ROOT, PEELED AND
CUT INTO 1-CM (½-IN) ROUND SLICES
(YOU COULD USE CANNED, DRAINED
LOTUS ROOT, IF NEEDED)

4 TEASPOONS SUNFLOWER OIL OR RAPESEED
(CANOLA) OIL

1 TEASPOON VER MASALA (PAGE 18)

300 G (10½ OZ) FRENCH (GREEN) BEANS,
WASHED AND HALVED

1 TEASPOONS SALT

1–2 TEASPOONS KASHMIRI CHILLI PASTE

1 TEASPOON GROUND GINGER

100 ML (3½ FL OZ/SCANT ½ CUP) HOT WATER

STEAMED RICE OR FLATBREADS, TO SERVE

KANAGUCHHI YAKHNI

MORELS IN SPICY YOGHURT GRAVY

SERVES 3–4

During my visit to Kashmir, I was very lucky to taste proper Kashmiri morels, which are rich, with a musky, strong flavour. Known locally as guchhi, *they grow wild in the Himalayan region and are expensive because they cannot be commercially cultivated. They can be bought online or in some speciality shops.*

Place the morels to soak in a bowl of lukewarm water for 15 minutes, then drain.

Heat the oil in a large pan over a medium heat. Once hot, add the cinnamon stick, cloves and cardamom pods, and fry for 1 minute. Add the drained morels and fry for another 3–4 minutes.

Add the crushed garlic and onion paste and cook for 2–3 minutes. Add the ground fennel and ginger, chilli powder, turmeric and salt. Mix well and cook for 1 minute. Reduce the heat, then stir in the whisked yoghurt mixture, stir and cook for a further 5 minutes.

Remove from the heat and stir through the black cumin seeds before serving with steamed rice.

INGREDIENTS

300 G (10½ OZ) DRIED MOREL MUSHROOMS, CLEANED

5 TEASPOONS MUSTARD OIL OR RAPESEED (CANOLA) OIL

8 CM (3 IN) CINNAMON STICK

4 WHOLE CLOVES

2 BLACK CARDAMOM PODS

4 GREEN CARDAMOM PODS

3 GARLIC CLOVES, CRUSHED TO A PASTE

2 TEASPOONS ONION PASTE OR SHALLOT PASTE (PAGE 17)

1 TABLESPOON GROUND FENNEL

2 TEASPOONS GROUND GINGER

1 TEASPOON KASHMIRI CHILLI POWDER

1 TEASPOON GROUND TURMERIC

1 TEASPOON SALT

100 G (3½ OZ/SCANT ½ CUP) GREEK YOGHURT, WHISKED WITH 400 ML (13 FL OZ/GENEROUS 1½ CUPS) WATER

1 TEASPOON BLACK CUMIN SEEDS

STEAMED RICE, TO SERVE

AAL YAKHNI (LAUKI)

BOTTLE GOURD/SUMMER SQUASH
COOKED IN YOGHURT

SERVES 4

Lauki (bottle gourd) was never my favourite vegetable while growing up, but then I had a very similar vegetable at my friend's house cooked in yoghurt. The texture grew on me, and since then I love cooking it in different ways. When cooking with yoghurt, you must cook over a low heat, and keep whisking so the yoghurt doesn't curdle.

Heat the ghee or oil in a large pan over a medium–high heat and fry the gourd or squash in batches, for 5–6 minutes, until light golden brown on all sides. Remove and set aside.

To the same pan, add the cinnamon stick, cloves, cardamom pods and cumin seeds, and cook for 1 minute. Add the crushed garlic and cook for another minute, then add the ground spices and salt and mix. Reduce the heat to low, add the whisked yoghurt and water, stir well and cook for 3 minutes. Add the fried gourd/squash and cook for a further 5–6 minutes until tender.

Stir through the black cumin seeds and leave to rest for 15 minutes before serving with rice.

INGREDIENTS

4 TEASPOONS GHEE OR 8 TEASPOONS MUSTARD OIL

500 G (1 LB 2 OZ) BOTTLE GOURD (LAUKI) OR SUMMER SQUASH, PEELED AND CUT INTO SMALL CHUNKS OR 2-CM (¾-IN) DISCS

8 CM (3 IN) CINNAMON STICK

3 WHOLE CLOVES

4 GREEN CARDAMOM PODS

2 BLACK CARDAMOM PODS

1 TEASPOON CUMIN SEEDS

6–8 GARLIC CLOVES, CRUSHED

1½ TEASPOONS GROUND GINGER

1½ TEASPOONS GROUND FENNEL

1 TEASPOON GROUND TURMERIC

1 TEASPOON SALT

150 G (5 OZ/SCANT ⅔ CUP) GREEK YOGHURT, WHISKED

500 ML (17 FL OZ/2 CUPS) WATER

½ TEASPOON BLACK CUMIN SEEDS

STEAMED RICE, TO SERVE

BOM CHOONTH TE WANGUN

QUINCE WITH AUBERGINES

SERVES 4

Popularly served at Hindu festivals as well as at normal day-to-day meals, this dish is only eaten when quinces are in season and is generally served as a side dish with other curries as well as rice.

Place the quince and aubergine chunks into 2 separate bowls and sprinkle each one with ¼ teaspoon of the salt and ½ teaspoon of the turmeric. Mix and set aside.

Heat the oil in a large pan over a high heat. Add the marinated vegetables – first the aubergine and then the quince – and cook for 5–6 minutes until light brown. Remove from the pan and set aside on a plate.

To the same pan, add the remaining spices and the remaining 1 teaspoon salt. Stir together, then add the water. Bring to the boil and cook for 5 minutes. Return the cooked vegetables to the pan, stir and cook on a medium heat for 15–20 minutes until tender.

INGREDIENTS

250 G (9 OZ) QUINCES, PEELED, CORED AND SLICED INTO HALF-MOONS

250 G (9 OZ) AUBERGINES (EGGPLANT) (IDEALLY SMALL, BUT YOU CAN USE LARGE), CUT INTO FINGERS

1½ TEASPOONS SALT

1 TEASPOON GROUND TURMERIC

8 TEASPOONS RAPESEED (CANOLA) OIL

1 TEASPOON GROUND GINGER

1 TEASPOON GROUND FENNEL

2 TEASPOONS KASHMIRI CHILLI POWDER

4 WHOLE CLOVES

1 TEASPOON GREEN CARDAMOM SEEDS, CRUSHED

½ TEASPOON ASAFOETIDA POWDER

250 ML (8½ FL OZ/1 CUP) WATER

BOM CHOONTH

QUINCE IN A TANGY SAUCE

SERVES 3–4

I was never aware of savoury quince dishes until I visited Kashmir – I have only ever made fruit leather, chutney and jelly with quinces in UK. This is the type of dish that gives the perfect flavour balance of sweet and tart to complement your other curries. It has become a regular in my house – we often eat it with dal and rice.

Heat the ghee or oil in a large pan over a high heat. Add the quince chunks and cook until light brown. Remove from the pan and set aside.

To the same pan, add the asafoetida powder, cinnamon stick, bay leaves and cardamom pods, and cook for 1 minute. Add the chilli paste and tamarind paste, along with the ground ginger, fennel, salt and sugar. Mix well, then add the hot water. Bring the mixture to the boil, then reduce the heat, add the cooked quince, cover and cook for 15–20 minutes until tender. After 15 minutes of cooking, stir through the cockscomb flower extract, if using.

Remove from the heat and stir through the black cumin seeds, just before serving.

INGREDIENTS

1 TABLESPOON GHEE OR 5 TEASPOONS MUSTARD OIL

500 G (1 LB 2 OZ) QUINCES, PEELED, CORED AND CUT INTO CHUNKS

½ TEASPOON ASAFOETIDA POWDER

8 CM (3 IN) CINNAMON STICK

2 BAY LEAVES

4 GREEN CARDAMOM PODS

2 TEASPOONS KASHMIRI CHILLI PASTE

2 TEASPOONS TAMARIND PASTE

2 TEASPOONS GROUND GINGER

½ TEASPOON GROUND FENNEL

1 TEASPOON SALT

2 TEASPOONS SUGAR

600 ML (20 FL OZ/2½ CUPS) HOT WATER

100 ML (3½ FL OZ/SCANT ½ CUP) COCKSCOMB FLOWER EXTRACT (PAGES 15–16) (OPTIONAL)

½ TEASPOONS BLACK CUMIN SEEDS

TAMATAR
TE WANGUN

AUBERGINES COOKED WITH TOMATOES

SERVES 3

When visiting Kashmir and Jammu, I saw that thin, long aubergines (eggplant) were popular dishes among the Kashmiri Hindus. I am a big fan of aubergines and learning to cook and eat them in different ways is exciting. The sweet, sour tomatoes work well with the aubergines here.

Place the aubergines into a large bowl and sprinkle with ½ teaspoon of the salt and the turmeric. Mix and set aside for 15 minutes.

Heat 5 teaspoons of the oil in a large pan over a medium heat and fry the marinated aubergines until light brown. Remove from the pan with a slotted spoon and set aside to drain on a plate lined with paper towels.

To the same pan, add the remaining 3 teaspoons of oil, then add the cumin seeds and asafoetida. When they start sizzling, add the chopped tomatoes and cook for 5–6 minutes until they are soft.

Add the ground ginger and chilli powder, along with the remaining ½ teaspoon of salt. Add the water and cook for 2 minutes, then return the fried aubergines to the pan. Add the green chillies and cook for another 5 minutes, stirring occasionally.

Remove from the heat and leave to rest for 30 minutes before serving with steamed rice.

INGREDIENTS

8 LONG THIN AUBERGINES (EGGPLANT)
(OR 2 LARGE ONES), QUARTERED LENGTHWAYS,
KEEPING THE STEM END INTACT SO THEY ARE
JOINED AT THE TOP

1 TEASPOON SALT

½ TEASPOON GROUND TURMERIC

8 TEASPOONS MUSTARD OIL OR
SUNFLOWER OIL

1 TEASPOON BROWN CUMIN SEEDS

½ TEASPOON ASAFOETIDA POWDER

500 G (1 LB 2 OZ) TOMATOES, CHOPPED

1 TEASPOON GROUND GINGER

2 TEASPOONS KASHMIRI CHILLI POWDER

100 ML (3½ FL OZ/SCANT ½ CUP) WATER

2–3 GREEN CHILLIES, HALVED
(DON'T REMOVE SEEDS)

STEAMED RICE, TO SERVE

CHOK WANGUN

SOUR AUBERGINES

SERVES 4

This recipe was given to me by Amit's mum, Rajni Wanchoo, and is the most popular dish among Kashmiri Pandits. No marriage is complete without these aubergines (eggplant) on the menu.

In a small bowl, dissolve the tamarind paste in the hot water and set aside.

Pour sunflower oil into a deep, heavy-based pan to a depth of 8 cm (3 in). Place over a medium heat and heat to 180°C/350°F on a digital thermometer. Alternatively, you can drop in a tiny piece of bread: if it sizzles and browns in 15 seconds, the oil is hot enough.

Once the oil is hot, carefully lower the aubergine slices into the oil and deep-fry for around 3 minutes until golden brown. Remove with a slotted spoon and set aside to drain on a plate lined with paper towels. You will need to do this in batches.

Heat the mustard or rapeseed oil in a frying pan (skillet) over a high heat. When hot, reduce the temperature to low and add the cumin seeds, bay leaves, cloves and asafoetida. Fry for 1 minute, then add the chilli powder and yoghurt, whisking to ensure the yoghurt doesn't curdle, and cook for another 2–3 minutes.

Stir through the sugar, salt, ground fennel and ginger, then add the tamarind water. Increase the heat and bring to the boil. Add the fried aubergines and boil for 2–3 minutes, then reduce the heat to medium and cook for a further 6–7 minutes.

Finally, stir through the ground cumin, ground black cardamom seeds and cinnamon, then serve with rice.

INGREDIENTS

40 G (1½ OZ/3 TABLESPOONS) TAMARIND PASTE

600 ML (20 FL OZ/2½ CUPS) HOT WATER

SUNFLOWER OIL, FOR DEEP-FRYING

300 G (10½ OZ) LONG, THIN AUBERGINES (EGGPLANT) (OR 2 LARGE), QUARTERED LENGTHWAYS, REMOVING THE STALKS

4 TEASPOONS MUSTARD OIL OR RAPESEED (CANOLA) OIL

1 TEASPOON CUMIN SEEDS

2–3 DRIED BAY LEAVES

3 WHOLE CLOVES

½ TEASPOON ASAFOETIDA POWDER

2 TEASPOONS KASHMIRI CHILLI POWDER

2 TEASPOONS GREEK YOGHURT

1 TEASPOON SUGAR

1 TEASPOON SALT

1½ TEASPOONS GROUND FENNEL

1 TEASPOON GROUND GINGER

1 TEASPOON GROUND CUMIN

1 BLACK CARDAMOM POD, SEEDS CRUSHED

½ TEASPOON GROUND CINNAMON

STEAMED RICE, TO SERVE

GOGJI

TURNIP CURRY

SERVES 4

Turnips in season just bring me sheer joy. I also love pickling and fermenting them. Learning that the same spices can be used in different ways was so eye-opening for me as a chef. The sweetness and meaty texture of the turnips, especially when fried in ghee and almost caramelised, makes a great vegetarian main dish, which is delicious served with rice.

Place the chopped turnips in a bowl and sprinkle with ½ teaspoon of the salt. Set aside for 20 minutes.

Heat the ghee or oil in a large pan over a high heat. Add the turnips and fry for 5 minutes until light brown. Remove from the pan with a slotted spoon and set aside on a plate.

To the same pan, add the cinnamon stick, cardamom pods, turmeric, chilli paste, garlic paste, shallot paste and hot water, along with the remaining ½ teaspoon of salt.

Bring the mixture to the boil, then cook over a medium heat for 6–7 minutes.

Once the water has reduced, add the fried turnips and cook until the turnips are soft, about 10 minutes. Mix in the black cumin seeds and cook for a final few minutes before removing from the heat to serve.

INGREDIENTS

500 G (1 LB 2 OZ) TURNIPS, PEELED AND CUT INTO 1 CM (½ IN) THICK DISCS, THEN QUARTERED

1 TEASPOON SALT

2 TABLESPOONS GHEE OR 6 TEASPOONS RAPESEED (CANOLA) OIL

8 CM (3 IN) CINNAMON STICK

4 GREEN CARDAMOM PODS

2 BLACK CARDAMOM PODS

1 TEASPOON GROUND TURMERIC

2 TEASPOONS KASHMIRI CHILLI PASTE

4 GARLIC CLOVES, CRUSHED TO A PASTE

1 TEASPOON SHALLOT PASTE (PAGE 17)

300 ML (10 FL OZ/1¼ CUPS) HOT WATER

½ TEASPOON BLACK CUMIN SEEDS

AAL POSH

SPICY PUMPKIN

SERVES 4

Pumpkins (squash) grown in India have a different taste to the ones in the UK. However, these spices work like magic and make them taste very similar. Any variety of squash can be used for this recipe, too.

Heat the oil in a large pan over a high heat. Add the pumpkin and fry for 4–5 minutes until golden brown on all sides. Remove with a slotted spoon and set aside on a plate.

To the same pan, add the asafoetida, ground ginger, fennel, cloves, black cardamom pods, chilli powder and salt, and mix well. Add the water and bring to the boil, then reduce the heat.

Add the whisked yoghurt and keep whisking until well combined. Return the fried pumpkin to the pan and cook for 10 minutes until the gravy thickens.

Mix in the ground cinnamon and crushed green cardamom seeds, then remove from the heat.

Serve with rice or flatbreads.

INGREDIENTS

2 TABLESPOONS RAPESEED (CANOLA) OIL

500 G (1 LB 2 OZ) PUMPKIN (SQUASH), PEELED AND CUT INTO 2 CM (¾ IN) PIECES

1 TEASPOON ASAFOETIDA POWDER

1 TEASPOON GROUND GINGER

1 TEASPOON GROUND FENNEL

½ TEASPOON GROUND CLOVES

2 BLACK CARDAMOM PODS

2 TEASPOONS KASHMIRI CHILLI POWDER

1 TEASPOON SALT

100 ML (3½ FL OZ/SCANT ½ CUP) WATER

100 G (3½ OZ/GENEROUS ⅓ CUP) GREEK YOGHURT, WHISKED

½ TEASPOON GROUND CINNAMON

3 GREEN CARDAMOM PODS, SEEDS CRUSHED

STEAMED RICE OR FLATBREADS, TO SERVE

WANGUN YAKHNI

FRIED AUBERGINES IN YOGHURT

SERVES 4

Here, aubergines (eggplant) are cooked in a delicious creamy yoghurt with a delicate balance of aromatic spices.

Pour sunflower oil into a deep, heavy-based pan to a depth of 8 cm (3 in). Place over a medium heat and heat to 180°C/350°F on a digital thermometer. Alternatively, you can drop in a tiny piece of bread: if it sizzles and browns in 15 seconds, the oil is hot enough.

Once the oil is hot, carefully lower the aubergine slices into the oil and deep-fry for 5 minutes until golden brown and crispy. Remove from the pan with a slotted spoon and set aside to drain on a plate lined with paper towels. You will need to do this in batches.

In a bowl, combine the yoghurt, water, turmeric, ginger, fennel and cumin, along with the clove powder. Whisk it all together and set aside.

Heat the 4 teaspoons of oil in a large pan over a low heat. Add the cinnamon stick and bay leaves, and cook for 1 minute. Add the salt and the whisked yoghurt mixture, and cook for 3 minutes, stirring continuously. Increase the heat to medium and add the fried aubergines. Cook for 8–10 minutes.

Just before serving, stir through the black cumin and ground cardamom seeds. Serve with rice.

INGREDIENTS

4 TEASPOONS SUNFLOWER OIL, PLUS EXTRA FOR DEEP-FRYING

500 G (1 LB 2 OZ) AUBERGINES (EGGPLANT), CUT IN HALF AND THEN INTO CHUNKY FINGERS

200 G (7 OZ/GENEROUS ¾ CUP) GREEK YOGHURT, WHISKED

100 ML (3½ FL OZ/SCANT ½ CUP) WATER

1 TEASPOON GROUND TURMERIC

1 TEASPOON GROUND GINGER

1½ TEASPOONS GROUND FENNEL

1 TEASPOON GROUND CUMIN

3 WHOLE CLOVES, CRUSHED TO A POWDER IN A PESTLE AND MORTAR

8 CM (3 IN) CINNAMON STICK

2 BAY LEAVES

1½ TEASPOONS SALT

½ TEASPOON BLACK CUMIN SEEDS

4 TEASPOONS CRUSHED GREEN CARDAMOM SEEDS

STEAMED RICE, TO SERVE

MAAZ

MEAT

Since childhood and now as a writer I have been very fascinated with *wazwan* and the meat dishes cooked in Kashmir. Food, in particular meat dishes, is at the heart of every celebration; there is nothing more joyous than when eating and sharing food together.

While travelling in Kashmir I didn't really eat many chicken dishes. The few I have included in this chapter are a collection of some of the recipes I sampled. Easy to make, the chicken recipes are, in a sense, a tribute to the food I ate there, learning from the wonderful people I met on my travels.

All the recipes in this chapter are a labour of love, using different techniques and methods. In some of these dishes it is worth taking the time to prepare the spices by hand – yes, you can us a blender but you won't get the same texture and taste as you would when using a pestle and mortar. The recipes in this section have been kindly shared with me by Hayat, Amit, Prateek, chefs from the various hotel restaurants I visted, Salim my guide and Younis, who was my driver from my second trip to Kashmir. I hope eating and cooking the recipes from my Himalayan travels will give you the same sense of pleasure and love that I received.

THE ULTIMATE KASHMIRI BANQUET

What better way to learn about a *wazwan* – Kashmir's sumptuous multi-course banquet –than to spend time with a *waza* – a chef who specialises in its preparation. I was privileged to be able to do this on one of my trips to Kashmir. If you ever get the chance to meet a *shaitan waza* (a member of a family of chefs known as the 'devil's chefs'), then you must. The expectation was that each son would follow in their father's footsteps and carry on this fascinating tradition. In Kashmir or any part of India, in fact, children – most often sons – would follow in the footsteps of their fathers.

Eaten at weddings and funerals – as well as at some restaurants – a *wazwan* is a true Kashmiri feast, comprising no fewer than 26–36 courses. Served on large metal trays known as *trami*, every course is served simultaneously, and the visual impact is equally as important as the flavours. Diners sit in groups of four on a sheet – *dastarkhwan* – on the floor, sharing the meal, traditionally eaten with the hands.

Thanks to the abundance of locally grown fresh herbs and spices, the dishes tend to be very rich in flavour but mild in terms of heat, with thick gravies that are slow-cooked for hours over fire, in a true labour of love.

Saffron is infused into many of the broths, for aroma, flavour and colour. It is found in savoury delicacies such as tender lamb *rogan josh*, with its vibrant red gravy, and *kokur* (chicken in a saffron sauce), as well as the creamy semolina milk pudding known as *phirin*, and melt-in-the-mouth *halwa*, which uses saffron to give it a stunning golden colour.

It's not just food that is an important use for saffron in Kashmir – it's a key ingredient in the region's best-known drink. Kashmiri *kahwa* sees green tea leaves brewed and infused with saffron, cinnamon and cardamom to create a warming drink with an intriguing flavour that is certainly an acquired taste. Depending on where you drink it and your own preferences, it may be sweetened with honey, sugar or different jams, and garnished with almonds. This was a drink that I was offered wherever I went during my time in Kashmir – and one on which I quickly became hooked.

AHDOOS RESTAURANT

Chef Thomas – a friend of mine who was formerly head chef at the Bombay Canteen in Mumbai – was instrumental in helping me to meet some of the region's most influential restaurateurs and chefs. It was he who introduced me to Hyaat: the grandson of the man who opened the historic Ahdoos Restaurant in Srinagar over a century ago, and the restaurant's current owner. It's a popular place to enjoy a *wazwan*, but its use has changed over the years. It originally began as a bakery (and the ground floor of the building still serves this purpose). It was named after the father of its founder.

When we visited, Ahdoos was heaving with locals and visitors alike – many of the latter staying at the hotel, which is the newest addition to the business. While we waited for our food, Hyaat expanded on the history of Ahdoos, which began life back in 1918. It was Hyaat's grandfather, Muhammad Sultan Bhat, who brought the vision to life, opening a shop in Polo View that sold tea, cakes and other treats to entice British people – its main customers before 1947. He told me how there was a band that played in the evenings, but after the partition – when the British population left Kashmir – the band left, too.

The meal that Hyaat had ordered for me was perfect: little bites of a range of dishes to try. A fragrant *methi maaz* (lamb offal with fenugreek), a *dhaniwal korma* (lamb in a yoghurt-based gravy with coriander), *rista* (meatballs in a rich, spicy, red gravy) and *mirchwangun korma* (a spicy dish that uses whole chillies, including the seeds) were all beautifully cooked, and showcased the different ways in which the Ahdoos team uses various cuts of meat from a single animal.

Over the years, Ahdoos has welcomed many famous people, and it's great to see a Srinagar business that has remained a success despite the region's decades of strife. In the 1990s, Ahdoos was the only hotel open all year round, which meant that for much of the year, it was teeming with news correspondents and television crews, keen to report the latest from the area.

I was also so glad to see that Hyaat has retained the bakery as part of Ahdoos. Bakery culture plays a unique role in Kashmir, and each city and town has many bakeries, catering to the needs of both Central Asian and British visitors. It's beautiful to see how the region's culture and heritage has been preserved through the means of baked goods. I visited several bakeries while I was there, and was amazed by the variety and authenticity of the breads, cakes and biscuits from different cultures that were on offer. Everything I tasted was delicious, and reflected Kashmir's diverse, rich and ancient history, ingredients and techniques. I can't wait to return and learn the art of bread making from these incredible people.

TABAKH MAAZ

FRIED RIBS

SERVES 4–5

Tabakh maaz is one of my favourite dishes. A Kashmiri delicacy, these crispy, delicate ribs are enjoyed at weddings, banquets and celebrations. They are usually eaten on their own, but can also be served as part of a trami, *a traditional arrangement of food, usually served on a large metal plate or platter, consisting of a varied selection of dishes served over a mound of rice.*

Put the rib pieces into a deep saucepan along with the water, garlic paste, cloves, cardamom pods, cinnamon stick, ginger, turmeric and salt, and mix well. Cook until tender and the meat is starting to come away from the bone, about 45 minutes. Once cooked, remove the ribs from the spicy water and discard the water.

Heat a separate pan over a high heat and add the cooked ribs, then pour the ghee over the meat. Fry for 10–12 minutes, until crispy and brown, turning them occasionally.

Serve hot.

INGREDIENTS

500 G (1 LB 2 OZ) RIBS (GOAT OR LAMB), CHOPPED INTO RECTANGULAR PIECES

1 LITRE (34 FL OZ/4 CUPS) WATER

20 G (¾ OZ) GARLIC, CRUSHED TO A PASTE

5 WHOLE CLOVES

4 BLACK CARDAMOM PODS

5 CM (2 IN) CINNAMON STICK

1 TEASPOON GROUND GINGER

1 TEASPOON GROUND TURMERIC

2 TEASPOONS SALT

5 TEASPOONS GHEE

HADIWALA MARCHWAGAN KORMA

RED HOT MEAT CURRY

SERVES 4

The simplicity of using the same spices in different combinations is what attracted me to the cuisine of Kashmir. This recipe includes a lot of different spices, but they're worth buying – you'll use them in plenty of Kashmiri dishes. With its super-tender meat on the bone, this dish is a great weekend feast. I loved this dish so much that I had to go back for seconds at Ahdoos restaurant.

Put the meat pieces into a deep saucepan along with the water, ½ teaspoon of the salt and the garlic paste, bring to the boil, then reduce the heat to medium and simmer until the meat is half cooked, about 25 minutes. Skim off and discard any scum that rises to the surface. Remove from the heat and strain the cooking water into a jug. Set the meat aside to cool.

Heat the ghee in a deep pan (you could use the same pan) over a high heat, then add the whole spices and cook for 1 minute. Add the cooked meat and fry for 3 minutes, then add the reserved cooking stock. Bring to the boil, then reduce the heat to low and add the chilli powder and ginger, and the remaining 1 teaspoon of salt. Cook, stirring occasionally, for 30 minutes.

To finish, stir through the black cumin seeds and cook for a final 3–4 minutes.

Serve with steamed rice.

INGREDIENTS

750 G (1 LB 10 OZ) LEG OF LAMB, CUT INTO 2 CM (¾ IN) PIECES

1 LITRE (34 FL OZ/4 CUPS) WATER

1½ TEASPOONS SALT

6 GARLIC CLOVES, CRUSHED TO A PASTE

5 TEASPOONS GHEE

8 CM (3 IN) CINNAMON STICK

4 WHOLE CLOVES

6 GREEN CARDAMOM PODS

2 BLACK CARDAMOM PODS

4–5 TEASPOONS KASHMIRI CHILLI POWDER

2 TEASPOONS GROUND GINGER

½ TEASPOON BLACK CUMIN SEEDS

STEAMED RICE, TO SERVE

DODHE MAAZ/ ABB GOSHT

LAMB COOKED IN MILK

SERVES 4–5

RECIPE BY HYAAT

Most Kashmiri dishes are made in the morning and eaten at night, so the flavours have time to infuse. I suggest leaving this curry to rest before serving to intensify its flavours, but how long you choose to rest it is up to you.

Put the meat in a deep saucepan over a high heat along with the water, cinnamon stick, bay leaves, cloves and 2 cardamom pods. Cook for 30 minutes until the meat is tender. Remove from the heat.

Pour the milk into a separate pan with the remaining 2 cardamom pods, and bring to the boil, then reduce the heat to medium and simmer until it is reduced by half. Set aside.

Heat the ghee in a deep pan over a medium heat. Add the garlic and shallot paste and cook for 1 minute, then add the salt, black pepper and ground fennel, and cook for 2 minutes. Add the meat and its cooking stock to the pan, stir well and bring to the boil. Add the reduced milk, then reduce the heat to medium and cook for a further 15–20 minutes until the sauce has thickened to your liking.

Leave to rest for at least an hour before serving. Eat with freshly cooked rice.

INGREDIENTS

800 G (1 LB 12 OZ) LAMB CUTLETS

500 ML (17 FL OZ/2 CUPS) WATER

5 CM (2 IN) CINNAMON STICK

2 BAY LEAVES

2 WHOLE CLOVES

4 GREEN CARDAMOM PODS

500 ML (17 FL OZ/2 CUPS) FULL-FAT (WHOLE) MILK

4 TEASPOONS GHEE

4 GARLIC CLOVES, CRUSHED

2 TEASPOONS SHALLOT PASTE (PAGE 17)

1 TEASPOON SALT

1 TEASPOON BLACK PEPPER

1 TEASPOON GROUND FENNEL

STEAMED RICE, TO SERVE

MUSLIM ROGAN JOSH

ROGAN JOSH

SERVES 6–7

This rogan josh *recipe is from the beautiful Kashmir Valley and is the Wafa Vakil's favourite – she was kind enough to describe it to me. It is very different to the one we are used to eating in the West – Kashmiri Muslims tend to use* praan, *a type of shallot, plus garlic and cockscomb flower for colouring. Kashmiri Hindus avoid shallots, but use asafoetida, spices and yoghurt for a greater depth of flavour.*

INGREDIENTS

1 KG (2 LB 4 OZ) BONE-IN LAMB LEG, CUT INTO PIECES ON THE BONE (ASK YOUR BUTCHER TO DO THIS FOR YOU, IF NECESSARY)

1 LITRE (34 FL OZ/4 CUPS) WATER

15 G (½ OZ) GARLIC, CRUSHED TO A PASTE

1½ TEASPOONS SALT

2 TABLESPOONS RAPESEED (CANOLA) OIL

5 CM (2 IN) CINNAMON STICK

4 WHOLE CLOVES

6 GREEN CARDAMOM PODS

2 BLACK CARDAMOM PODS

3 DRIED BAY LEAVES

2 TEASPOONS GROUND FENNEL

2 TEASPOONS GROUND GINGER

2 TEASPOONS GROUND TURMERIC

½ TEASPOON FRESHLY GROUND BLACK PEPPER

4 TEASPOONS SHALLOT PASTE (PAGE 17)

1 TABLESPOON KASHMIRI CHILLI POWDER DISSOLVED IN 3 TABLESPOONS WATER

200 ML (7 FL OZ/SCANT 1 CUP) COCKSCOMB FLOWER EXTRACT (PAGES 15–16) (OPTIONAL)

½ TEASPOON SAFFRON STRANDS SOAKED IN 4 TEASPOONS LUKEWARM WATER

STEAMED RICE, TO SERVE

Put the meat in a deep saucepan along with the water, crushed garlic and ½ teaspoon of the salt. Boil for 20 minutes until the meat is half cooked. Skim off and discard any scum that rises to the surface. Remove from the heat and strain the cooking stock into a jug. Set the meat aside.

Heat the oil in a large pan with a lid over a medium heat. Add the whole spices and bay leaves and cook for 1 minute, then add all the ground spices, along with the remaining 1 teaspoon of salt, the shallot paste and the chilli powder in its soaking water. Stir continuously until well combined. Increase the heat to high and add the boiled meat. Sauté for about 4 minutes, then reduce the heat to low. Add the reserved cooking stock, cover and cook for 30–35 minutes until the meat is tender.

Add the cockscomb flower extract (if using) and the soaked saffron. Mix well, and cook for a final 2 minutes.

Serve piping hot with rice.

MATZ CHHIEAR

MEATBALLS STUFFED WITH APRICOTS

SERVES 4

This recipe was introduced to me by my dearest chef friend, Prateek. These tender meatballs, flavoured with sweet dried apricots, chilli and spices, are the perfect combination of sweet and savoury and one of many savoury dishes to use this popular Kashmiri fruit. Serve with hot rice or your favourite freshly baked Kashmiri bread.

Put the minced lamb in a food processor and blitz to a smooth texture.

Transfer the resulting meat paste into a bowl, and add ½ teaspoon each of the ground ginger, fennel, cumin, black cardamom seeds, chilli powder and salt, along with 2 teaspoons of the oil. Mix well, then divide the mixture into equal portions, then roll each one into a ball around the size of a golf ball. Stuff 5–6 pieces of chopped apricots into the middle of each ball, making sure the apricots are completely enclosed. Place all the meatballs on a tray and refrigerate for 30 minutes.

Meanwhile, heat the remaining 2 teaspoons of oil in a large, wide saucepan over a medium heat. Once hot, add the bay leaves and cinnamon stick. As soon as they start to sizzle, mix in the asafoetida, then add the remaining ground spices and salt, plus the turmeric and ground cloves, and cook for 1 minute. Add the water and bring the mixture to the boil, then cook over a medium heat for about 10 minutes.

Add the meatballs to the gravy and cook for about 15 minutes until cooked through and the gravy has thickened. Serve with rice or flatbreads.

INGREDIENTS

500 G (1 LB 2 OZ) MINCED (GROUND) LAMB

2 TEASPOONS GROUND GINGER

2 TEASPOONS GROUND FENNEL

1 TEASPOON GROUND CUMIN

4 TEASPOONS GROUND BLACK CARDAMOM SEEDS

2 TEASPOONS KASHMIRI CHILLI POWDER

1½ TEASPOONS SALT

4 TEASPOONS SUNFLOWER OIL OR RAPESEED (CANOLA) OIL

150 G (5 OZ) DRIED APRICOTS, SOAKED IN HOT WATER FOR 30 MINUTES, THEN DRAINED AND FINELY DICED

2 BAY LEAVES

5 CM (2 IN) CINNAMON STICK

½ TEASPOON ASAFOETIDA POWDER

½ TEASPOON GROUND TURMERIC

½ TEASPOON GROUND CLOVES

750 ML (25 FL OZ/3 CUPS) WATER

STEAMED RICE OR FLATBREADS, TO SERVE

WAFA VAKIL
& CAFE LIBERTY

My next trip was to meet the beautiful Wafa (also known as Haya Vakil to many), one of the valley's first female radio DJs. I know what it's like to be the first female in a particular field – and I was keen to hear the experiences of someone who had weaved a path for other women to follow in a different sector.

It was back in 2006 that Wafa auditioned for a new Srinagar radio station that was about to launch. What may surprise some is that it was her parents who encouraged her to audition for the role, with her father in particular being a believer in women working to break glass ceilings and become known in fields more often dominated by men.

In 2019, after 13 years at the radio station, Wafa left to pursue a new business venture: opening Cafe Liberty in Srinagar, with her husband Khawar Jamsheed. Her dream was to create a space where people could not only enjoy great food, but could do so in a truly relaxed atmosphere, feeling completely comfortable whether just

sitting and eating with friends or family, or engrossed in a good book. Thanks to COVID-19 – as well as curfews imposed as a result of the political struggles in Kashmir, and the region's harsh climates – Wafa hasn't had an easy ride. Closure for any period of time, for any business, hits both running costs and profits hard, especially one that is still finding its feet. During my trip, though, Cafe Liberty was open.

The approach reminded me of Mumbai. Before even taking the lift to the cafe itself, the signage and the views through the windows gave the place that busy, trendy vibe that I've come to associate with the Maharashtrian capital. Not only does Wafa serve traditional Kashmiri food, but diners can also order more Western dishes such as pizzas, burgers and chips. She firmly believes that food should not have borders, and the cafe provides the younger generation with hope, fun and a relaxation of cultural boundaries. We chatted a while over traditional kebabs and pastries – a red velvet and a pineapple pastry version, both of which were more like light and fluffy sponge cakes than what we would describe as pastries in the UK.

Wafa told me that she had personally never felt discriminated against, in either her career as a radio DJ or as a cafe owner. Of course, she added, that does not mean that discrimination and favouritism do not exist. She has a tenacious desire to achieve everything she sets her mind to, and I see a lot of myself in her. I truly admire her outlook and her work ethic, and I can't wait to meet up with her again during future travels.

KONG KOKUR

SAFFRON CHICKEN

SERVES 4–5

While visiting Kashmir, I learnt so much about the food, people and the landscape. Although I had chicken on my travels, it wasn't widely served. I had a conversation about chicken dishes with Amit and Hayat, and they said people likely cook chicken at home with the same ingredients used in the lamb or vegetarian dishes. Using this as my inspiration, when I returned to the UK, I made a whole roasted chicken recipe using the Kashmiri spices for my family and friends to enjoy.

Preheat the oven to 200°C (180°C fan/400°F/gas 6).

Heat 5 teaspoons of the oil or ghee in a large pan, add the shallots and fry until golden brown, then remove from the heat and leave to cool. Once cool, blitz to a paste in a food processor.

Place all the whole and ground spices, along with the salt, in a spice grinder or pestle and mortar, and grind to a fine powder.

In a bowl, combine this spice powder with the shallot paste and saffron water, along with the remaining 3 teaspoons of oil or ghee. Mix together with a fork. Apply this spice paste to the whole chicken, ensuring it is thoroughly covered, then leave to marinate at room temperature for 30 minutes.

Place the marinated chicken in a roasting tray (pan) and roast in the hot oven for 1 hour 20 minutes.

Turn off the oven and leave the chicken to rest in the oven while you preheat the grill (broiler) to high.

Place the chicken under the grill and cook for 15 minutes until browned on top. Serve with chutneys or relishes of your choice, rice and any vegatarian side dish.

INGREDIENTS

8 TEASPOONS SUNFLOWER OIL OR GHEE

100 G (3½ OZ) SHALLOTS, THINLY SLICED

8 WHOLE CLOVES

8 CM (3 IN) CINNAMON STICK

2 TEASPOONS KASHMIRI CHILLI POWDER

2 TEASPOONS GROUND FENNEL

2 TEASPOONS GROUND GINGER

1 TEASPOON SALT

2 TEASPOONS SAFFRON STRANDS, SOAKED IN 3 TABLESPOONS LUKEWARM WATER

1 X 1 KG (2 LB 4 OZ) WHOLE CHICKEN, SKIN REMOVED

CHUTENEYS, RELISHES, RICE OR VEGETARIAN SIDE DISH, TO SERVE (OPTIONAL)

GHUSHTABA

POUNDED MUTTON MEATBALLS
IN A YOGHURT GRAVY

SERVES 4

Often served at wedding celebrations and restaurants, ghushtaba *is also an important part of the* wazwan. *Simple meatballs are simmered in a yoghurt-based gravy, in a flavoursome dish known by Kashmiri Muslims as 'The Dish of Kings'.*

For the meatballs, remove any fat from the meat and reserve the bones for the stock. Cut the meat into pieces and rub with ½ teaspoon of the salt. Place the meat on a wooden board (or smooth stone) and pound with a wooden mallet. Remove any pieces of sinew and keep pounding until the texture and colour of the meat resembles pâté. Add the lard, ghee or oil and continue to pound. Finally, add the remaining ½ teaspoon of salt and pound until everything is well combined and the meat has a paste-like texture. Alternatively, use a food processor to blitz it all to a fine paste. Divide the mixture and shape into 4 large balls with wet hands.

For the stock, place the bones in a large pan and add the water, cardamom pods, cloves, cinnamon and salt. Bring to the boil, then reduce to a simmer and cook for 30 minutes, until the stock is reduced by half to 500 ml (17 fl oz/2 cups). Remove and discard any scum that comes to the top. Once reduced, set aside.

To make the gravy, heat the ghee or oil in a separate large pan over a low heat. Add the whisked yoghurt and cook for 5 minutes, whisking continuously so that the mixture doesn't curdle. Add the crushed garlic and shallot paste, along with the ground ginger and fennel. Now, add the meatballs, and cook for 10 minutes, stirring.

Add the stock and cook for a further 15 minutes until the gravy thickens. Mix in the dried mint and leave to rest for 30 minutes. Resting helpings the broth to seep in the meat balls,

Serve hot, with steamed rice.

FOR THE MEATBALLS

600 G (1 LB 5 OZ) GOAT, MUTTON OR LAMB LEG (BUY IT ON THE BONE AND KEEP THE BONES FOR THE STOCK)

1 TEASPOON SALT

1 TABLESPOON LARD, GHEE OR RAPESEED (CANOLA) OIL

FOR THE STOCK

STOCK BONES (SEE ABOVE)

1 LITRE (34 FL OZ/4 CUPS) WATER

6 GREEN CARDAMOM PODS

4 BLACK CARDAMOM PODS

4 WHOLE CLOVES

5 CM (2 IN) CINNAMON STICK

1 TEASPOON SALT

FOR THE GRAVY

2 TABLESPOONS GHEE OR RAPESEED (CANOLA) OIL

600 G (1 LB 5 OZ/2½ CUPS) GREEK YOGHURT WHISKED WITH 300 ML (10 FL OZ/1¼ CUPS) WATER

6 GARLIC CLOVES, CRUSHED TO A PASTE

2 TEASPOONS SHALLOT PASTE (PAGE 17)

2 HEAPED TEASPOONS GROUND GINGER

2 HEAPED TEASPOONS GROUND FENNEL

500 ML (17 FL OZ/2 CUPS) STOCK (SEE ABOVE)

½ TEASPOON DRIED MINT

STEAMED RICE, TO SERVE

RISTA

MEATBALLS IN RED SAUCE

SERVES 3–4

This hearty, mildly-spiced dish is an important part of the wazwan *with beautiful warming flavours of saffron and cardamom. Cockscomb flower extract, if using, will give it a deep, rich red colour, a beautiful contrast to the steamed rice it is typically served with.*

First, make the meatballs and stock according to the method on page 107, rolling the balls much smaller so that you get 10 meatballs from the mixture, and reducing the stock a little less.

For the sauce, heat the ghee in a large pan with a lid over a high heat. Add the shallot and garlic paste, and cook for 10–12 minutes, stirring. Add the meatballs, stock, salt, cardamom pods, cloves, chilli paste and turmeric, and stir well. Reduce the heat to medium, cover and cook for 15–20 minutes until the meatballs are tender.

Add the saffron, cockscomb flower extract (if using) and black pepper and cook for a final 2 minutes.

Leave to rest for 30 minutes for serving.

INGREDIENTS

10 MEATBALLS (MADE ACCORDING TO THE METHOD ON PAGE 107) PLUS 600 ML (20 FL OZ/2½ CUPS) STOCK FROM THE BONES (PAGE 107)

STEAMED RICE, TO SERVE

FOR THE SAUCE

7 TEASPOONS GHEE OR RAPESEED (CANOLA) OIL

2 TABLESPOONS SHALLOT PASTE (PAGE 17)

6 GARLIC CLOVES, CRUSHED TO A PASTE

1 TEASPOON SALT

10 GREEN CARDAMOM PODS

4 WHOLE CLOVES

2 TEASPOONS KASHMIRI CHILLI PASTE

2 TEASPOONS GROUND TURMERIC

½ TEASPOON SAFFRON STRANDS SOAKED IN 4 TEASPOONS LUKEWARM WATER

2 TEASPOONS COCKSCOMB FLOWER EXTRACT (PAGES 15–16) (OPTIONAL)

½ TEASPOON FRESHLY GROUND BLACK PEPPER

KANAGUCHHI GOSHT

LAMB AND MOREL YAKHNI

SERVES 4–5

RECIPE BY PRATEEK

This recipe was kindly given to me by my lovely chef friend, Prateek Sadhu. Kanaguchhi – morel mushrooms – are an expensive ingredient in Kashmir, making this a fantastic celebration dish. The earthiness of the dried mushrooms gives it a wonderful depth of flavour.

Soak the dried morels in 300–400 ml (10–13 fl oz/ 1¼–1½ cups) water, enough so that they are fully submerged, for 1 hour, or until soft. Drain, reserving the soaking liquid.

In a bowl, combine the yoghurt, ground fennel and ginger, along with 100 ml (3½ fl oz/scant ½ cup) of the reserved morel-soaking liquid and mix together until smooth. Set aside.

Place the lamb in a large pan along with the measured water. Bring to the boil, then reduce the heat to medium and cook for 30 minutes. Remove and discard any scum that comes to the top. Drain, reserving 200 ml (7 fl oz/ scant 1 cup) of the resulting stock.

Heat the ghee and oil in a separate large pan over a medium heat. Once hot, add the whole spices and bay leaves and cook for 1 minute until fragrant. Add the shallots and cook, stirring, for another 10 minutes, then add the lamb, along with the salt, and sear lightly. Reduce the heat and slowly add the yoghurt mixture, whisking continuously until evenly combined. Finally, add the drained morels and reserved meat stock and simmer over a low heat for 10 minutes, stirring occasionally.

Serve with steamed rice and a vegetarian side dish of your choice.

INGREDIENTS

100 G (3½ OZ) DRIED MORELS (OR MIXED DRIED MUSHROOMS)

200 G (7 OZ/GENEROUS ¾ CUP) GREEK YOGHURT, WHISKED

4 TABLESPOONS GROUND FENNEL

3 TABLESPOONS GROUND GINGER

600 G (1 LB 5 OZ) LAMB LEG, DICED

300 ML (10 FL OZ/1¼ CUPS) WATER

50 G (2 OZ) GHEE

4 TEASPOONS RAPESEED (CANOLA) OIL

4–5 GREEN CARDAMOM PODS

2–3 BLACK CARDAMOM PODS

4–5 WHOLE BLACK PEPPERCORNS

2 TEASPOONS FENNEL SEEDS

2 BAY LEAVES

100 G (3½ OZ) SHALLOTS, FINELY CHOPPED

1 TEASPOON SALT

STEAMED RICE AND ANY VEGETARIAN SIDE DISH OF YOUR CHOICE, TO SERVE

A TRIP TO THE OLD CITY

My first stop on my tour of the old city of Srinagar was Jama Masjid, Kashmir's central mosque and the pride of the city. I wasn't sure whether I would be allowed to enter, but I was pleased to find that I could go inside to say a few prayers in this beautiful, peaceful place. At 14,170 square metres and able to hold around 30,000 devotees for a single prayer congregation – nearly 100,000 if the central courtyard is also used – it's an enormous place. Commissioned by Sultan Sikandar, it took eight years to build, and remains just as popular now – both for Friday prayers and for tourism – as it was when completed in 1402 CE.

Each of the mosque's four minarets is supported by eight columns, each made from a single deodar tree trunk. The minarets have open wooden pavilion, offering great viewpoints over Srinagar city, across to the Hari Parbat hill, and down to the city's small lanes and bazaar.

I was awed by the simplicity and calmness that I found surrounded by the hustle and bustle of the city's bazaar, it was the perfect place to reflect on myself and my situation. It helped me to get closer to the peace I have been missing since I lost my mum.

It felt surreal walking out of such a serene environment into the market, but I was a woman on a mission: I needed to visit the spice vendors to buy some dried cockscomb flower so that I could make the extract needed for some of my recipes, and I was also keen to explore the city's butcher shops. We weaved our way through stalls selling all sorts of foodstuffs: all manner of fresh vegetables; vibrant Kashmiri chillies; dried vegetables including bottle gourds, turnips and other vegetables sold in the jute bags.

It was a beautifully warm day – a pleasant warmth that meant I was happy to take my time and soak up as much of both the atmosphere and the sunshine as possible. We eventually reached the part of the market where all the exquisite traditional Kashmiri copper utensils are sold. India as a whole has a wealth of heritage, but there's nowhere quite like Kashmir when it comes to local handicrafts. According to some, it was Sufi saint and Islamic scholar Mir Syed Ali Hamdani who introduced copper work to the region in the 14th century. Travelling to Kashmir three times from Central Asia, he brought with him craftsmen to teach the locals how to make copperware, known as *kandkari*. It is a laborious process, with a number of artisans – blacksmiths, engravers, gilders, polishers – each playing their own important role in the process.

I left for Dargah Hazratbal, a holy shrine of utmost importance to all Muslims, lying on the left bank of the Dal Lake. It is a place filled with essence and love, and with the shimmering lake and houseboats nearby, it's a serene and relaxing spot to sit and watch the world go by. I said my prayers and made my way over to the nearby food stalls where I feasted on *halwa* – an almost porridge-like dish of oats cooked with milk, ghee and warming spices – as well as rich and delicious deep-fried *roti*. It was also an opportunity to try *nadru monje* – lotus root fritters – for the first time: a popular Kashmiri street snack where the crunchy stems are dredged in rice flour, cumin and Kashmiri chillies before being deep-fried.

Out of the corner of my eye, I spotted a man selling something in jute bags from his bike. Intrigued, I headed over, and he explained it was simply *rajma* – kidney beans – boiled in water, with a sprinkling of chillies and spices. It was proof that sometimes the simplest of dishes can be the best.

I walked for a while to clear my head, my current experiences jostling for space with memories of my younger years. The Kashmir I had once seen on my family's black-and-white TV was now a reality, and I found myself thinking of my parents. My mother had been desperate to travel to Kashmir, but all of their money was spent on us children and our education, with hardly any to spare for expensive holidays. Then my mother developed cancer and everything shattered for us. As she has now passed, I couldn't fulfil my promise of taking her on that longed-for journey to Kashmir, but I know she was there with me in spirit – and I know she will be so proud of me for writing this book.

BOTTOM

The Hazratbal Shrine, popularly called Dargah Sharif 'the Holy Shrine'. It is considered to be Kashmir's holiest Muslim shrine.

KALEJI TCHOKH CHARVAN

SPICY LIVER

SERVES 4

This recipe was given to me by my lovely driver, Younis. Lamb liver is traditionally used for this dish, which is served in a rich gravy. Don't forget the tamarind paste, as that tangy flavour is needed to cut through the richness of the meat. Generally, Kashmiris will only eat small portions of this dish, as it takes longer than other main courses to digest. I add fresh shallots rather than onions or shallot paste, as is the norm in Kashmir. Serve with rice or any flatbread.

Place the liver in a pan over a medium heat, along with the measured water for 20 minutes and boil until soft. Drain and set aside.

Heat the oil or ghee in a large pan with a lid over a high heat. Add the cloves and asafoetida and cook for 1 minute, then add the sliced shallots and cook for 10–12 minutes until browned. Add the boiled liver and fry for 3–4 minutes. Reduce the heat, then add the chilli powder, ground fennel, ginger, turmeric and salt, and cook for another 2 minutes, stirring to combine.

Finally, add the tamarind water and bring to the boil, then reduce the heat to medium, cover and cook for 15–20 minutes until the liver is soft and tender.

Remove from the heat and mix in the crushed black cardamom seeds. Leave to rest for at least 15 minutes before serving.

INGREDIENTS

500 G (1 LB 2 OZ) LIVER, CUT INTO 1 CM (½ IN) CUBES

500 ML (17 FL OZ/2 CUPS) WATER

2 TABLESPOONS RAPESEED (CANOLA) OIL OR 4 TEASPOONS GHEE

2 WHOLE CLOVES

½ TEASPOON ASAFOETIDA POWDER

200 G (7 OZ) SHALLOTS, THINLY SLICED

2 TEASPOONS KASHMIRI CHILLI POWDER

2 TEASPOONS GROUND FENNEL

1 TEASPOON GROUND GINGER

1 TEASPOON GROUND TURMERIC

1 TEASPOON SALT

2 TEASPOONS TAMARIND PASTE SOAKED IN 200 ML (7 FL OZ/SCANT 1 CUP) WATER

1 TEASPOON CRUSHED BLACK CARDAMOM SEEDS

MEETHI MAAZ

KASHMIRI OFFAL DELICACY

SERVES 4

A true wazwan *showcases dishes made with all different parts of the animal, including the offal. A good butcher will be able to source and prepare goat or lamb intestines for you to use in this dish – it's an affordable cut of meat with a buttery texture and a rich, meaty flavour.*

Thoroughly wash the offal under cold running water. To ensure it is all properly cleaned, wash at least 4–5 times. When thoroughly clean, place in a large pan, cover with the water and bring to the boil. Cook for 30–35 minutes, until the stock is clear, skimming off and discarding any scum that rises to the surface. When the stock is clear, add ½ teaspoon of the salt, along with the crushed garlic and all the whole spices, and simmer for 20 minutes.

Remove the intestines from the stock to a chopping board and leave to cool, then finely chop.

Place the stock back on the heat and add the remaining 1 teaspoon of salt, along with the ground ginger, chilli powder and turmeric. Add the minced intestines and cook over a medium heat for 20 minutes.

Meanwhile, heat the ghee in a separate small pan over a medium heat. Add the soaked fenugreek leaves and fry for 2 minutes, along with the crushed black cardamom seeds. Pour into the stock pan, mix well and cook for a further 3–4 minutes.

Serve hot with rice.

INGREDIENTS

1 KG (2 LB 4 OZ) GOAT OR LAMB INTESTINES (ASK YOUR BUTCHER TO OPEN THEM)

1 LITRE (34 FL OZ/4 CUPS) HOT WATER, OR ENOUGH TO COVER

1½ TEASPOONS SALT

10 GARLIC CLOVES, CRUSHED TO A PASTE

8 CM (3 IN) CINNAMON STICK

4 BLACK CARDAMOM PODS

6 GREEN CARDAMOM PODS

2 TEASPOONS GROUND GINGER

2 TEASPOONS KASHMIRI CHILLI POWDER

2 TEASPOONS GROUND TURMERIC

4 TEASPOONS GHEE

15 G (½ OZ/GENEROUS ½ CUP) DRIED FENUGREEK LEAVES (KASURI METHI), SOAKED IN HOT WATER FOR 15 MINUTES, THEN DRAINED

1 TEASPOON CRUSHED BLACK CARDAMOM SEEDS

STEAMED RICE, TO SERVE

NAAT YAKKHN

GOAT COOKED IN YOGHURT

SERVES 4

On my trip, Hayaat and I chatted about our love of food. He asked me which dishes were my favourite. I enjoyed them all very much but my favourite has to be Naat Yakkhn. *Traditionally this is cooked with lamb, but we used goat, here. This delicious yoghurt-based meat dish includes plenty of ghee, but it's surprisingly light on the stomach.*

Place the goat or lamb in a pan along with the measured water and ½ teaspoon of the salt and bring to the boil for 20 minutes. Skim off and discard any scum that rises to the surface. When the water is clear, add the crushed garlic and the whole spices and cook for a further 30 minutes over a medium heat.

Add the ghee to the pan, along with the ground ginger and turmeric, the remaining 1 teaspoon of salt, the chilli paste, the whisked yoghurt and the shallot paste. Whisk thoroughly and reduce the heat to low, then cover and cook for 20–30 minutes until the meat is tender.

Add the cockscomb flower extract (if using), black cumin seeds and dried mint and cook for a further 2 minutes. Remove from the heat and leave to rest for 1 hour before eating.

Serve hot with rice or flatbreads.

INGREDIENTS

500 G (1 LB 2 OZ) BONE-IN GOAT
OR LAMB LEG MEAT, DICED INTO CHUNKS

1 LITRE (34 FL OZ/4 CUPS) WATER

1½ TEASPOONS SALT

10 G (½ OZ) GARLIC, CRUSHED TO A PASTE

4 GREEN CARDAMOM PODS

2 BLACK CARDAMOM PODS

4 WHOLE CLOVES

4 TEASPOONS GHEE

1 TEASPOON GROUND GINGER

2 TEASPOONS GROUND TURMERIC

2 TEASPOONS KASHMIRI CHILLI PASTE

150 G (5 OZ/SCANT ⅔ CUP) GREEK YOGHURT,
WHISKED

2 TABLESPOONS SHALLOT PASTE (PAGE 17)

75 ML (2½ FL OZ/5 TABLESPOONS) COCKSCOMB
FLOWER EXTRACT (PAGES 15–16) (OPTIONAL)

½ TEASPOON BLACK CUMIN SEEDS

1 TEASPOON DRIED MINT

STEAMED RICE OR FLATBREADS, TO SERVE

HAAKH TE MAAZ

MUTTON WITH SPINACH

SERVES 4

Many will be familiar with the lamb saag that appears on Indian restaurant menus across the world. The Kashmiri version is somewhat simpler, but equally delicious.

I had this dish on my first trip to Srinagar, at the hotel I was staying at. The chefs there were so welcoming and were very open to share the way they cook. They told me that some people might not add tomatoes and that fish can sometimes be used instead of meat.

Place the spinach and measured water in a large pan, bring to the boil and cook for 4 minutes until the spinach is soft. Strain the cooking water into a jug, and set the spinach aside to cool. When cool, mash the spinach and set aside.

Heat the oil in a large pan over a medium heat. Add the asafoetida and dried chillies, and cook for 1 minute, then add the ground ginger and turmeric, mixing well. Increase the heat to high, then add the mutton and cook until browned all over.

Reduce the heat to low, then add the tomatoes and cook for 4–5 minutes. Add the reserved spinach cooking water, then cover and cook, still over a low heat, for about 30 minutes, stirring occasionally, until the meat is tender.

Add the mashed spinach and salt. Mix well and cook for a final 8–10 minutes. Sprinkle over the black cumin seeds, before removing from heat.

Leave to rest for an hour and reheat before serving with rice or flatbreads.

INGREDIENTS

1 KG (2 LB 4 OZ) SPINACH, WASHED, STEMS REMOVED

500 ML (17 FL OZ/2 CUPS) WATER

3 TABLESPOONS RAPESEED (CANOLA) OIL

½ TEASPOON ASAFOETIDA POWDER

4 DRIED WHOLE KASHMIRI CHILLIES

2 TEASPOONS GROUND GINGER

1 TEASPOON GROUND TURMERIC

750 G (1 LB 10 OZ) BONELESS MUTTON, CUT INTO 2-CM (¾-IN) CHUNKS

250 G (9 OZ) TOMATOES, CHOPPED

1½ TEASPOONS SALT

½ TEASPOON BLACK CUMIN SEEDS

STEAMED RICE OR FLATBREADS, TO SERVE

ALU BUKARA KORMA

LAMB WITH DRIED PLUMS

SERVES 4

This recipe was inspired by my many conversations with Amit. Spicy, tangy and full of flavour, this sweet and sour dish has dried plums (or prunes) and tamarind as the star of the show. Its flavour is incredibly deep and rich – it'll be unlike any dish you've tried before.

Soak the dried plums/prunes in lukewarm water for 30 minutes, then drain and set aside.

Heat the oil in a large pan with a lid over a high heat, add the cinnamon stick, cloves and crushed cardamom seeds and cook for 1 minute, then add the lamb and cook for 5–6 minutes until browned all over.

Add the chilli powder, ginger, turmeric, salt, garlic paste, shallot paste and tamarind water, along with the drained dried plums. Bring to the boil, then reduce the heat, cover and cook for 30–45 minutes until the meat is tender and the gravy has thickened.

Leave to rest for at least 1 hour. Reheat before serving with steamed rice.

INGREDIENTS

200 G (7 OZ) DRIED PLUMS/PRUNES, WASHED

2 TABLESPOONS RAPESEED (CANOLA) OIL

5 CM (2 IN) CINNAMON STICK

4 WHOLE CLOVES

4 GREEN CARDAMOM PODS, SEEDS CRUSHED

500 G (1 LB 2 OZ) BONELESS LEG OF LAMB, CUT INTO 2 CM (¾ IN) CHUNKS

2 TEASPOONS KASHMIRI CHILLI POWDER

1 TEASPOON GROUND GINGER

1 TEASPOON GROUND TURMERIC

1 TEASPOON SALT

10 G (½ OZ) GARLIC, CRUSHED TO A PASTE

2 TEASPOONS SHALLOT PASTE (PAGE 17)

2 TEASPOONS TAMARIND PASTE, DISSOLVED IN 500 ML (17 FL OZ/2 CUPS) WATER

STEAMED RICE, TO SERVE

A STORY OF NOON CHAI & HARISSA

I'd been introduced to Roohi Nazki, owner of Srinagar tearoom Chai Jaai, by my wonderful chef friend, Prateek Sadhu, before I had even planned my trip to Kashmir. She was keen for me to visit Chai Jaai, which she opened in 2016 as more of a passion project than a money-making venture. When I stepped out of the car, I was given such a warm welcome that it felt like we had known each other since childhood. I'd had no idea what to expect from the place, but I could never have conjured up this stunning contemporary building, its walls hand-painted by a local craftsman in the traditional Kashmiri *naquashi* style, with views across the Jhelum River.

Roohi's aim was to create an English-style tearoom, and she actually took her inspiration from the Cotswolds. Fusing both English and Kashmiri tea traditions, I was surprised to see red velvet cake, chocolate truffle cake and other British favourites on the menu, but I stuck to some popular Kashmiri recipes that Roohi was keen for me to try.

We began with *girda* – a flatbread made from fermented dough that is cooked in a tandoor – served with Kashmiri *harissa*. While many of us know harissa as the name for a fragrant red Tunisian chilli paste, the Kashmiri word refers to something completely different. The *harissa* I enjoyed at Chai Jaai was a traditional mutton recipe, mostly available in winter, which takes around 12 hours to cook with the meat drowning in the flavours of cinnamon, cardamom, fennel and more overnight. This fragrant, hearty dish is often served at family brunches, and it's one of the rarest and creamiest dishes I've eaten.

Next came the delicious *kahwa*: tea that Roohi had made by steeping green tea leaves with Kashmir-grown saffron strands, cardamom pods and cinnamon (some may also add rose petals). She served it sprinkled with chopped almonds and with two breads on the side. She recounted how *kahwa* is traditionally prepared in a copper kettle known as a *samavar*. It features a special container for coals inside, as well as a space in which water can boil, and the *kahwa* ingredients are added. *Samavars* are not cheap, but a good-quality purchase will last you for years. If like me, you simply don't own one, you can make *kahwah* in an ordinary saucepan.

While we chatted about the situation in Kashmir, the food and drink kept flowing. Next came *noon chai* and *makki di roti*: the former another traditional Kashmiri tea, the latter delicious maize-flour flatbreads with a wonderfully creamy, buttery texture. *Noon chai* is an incredibly striking drink, also cooked in a *samavar*, made with gunpowder tea, milk, salt and baking soda. It sounds unusual, I agree, but with its salty-sweet flavour and its vivid pink colour (the result of a reaction between the baking soda and the tea leaves), it's a perfect drink for the cold winter months. If you do make it yourself at home, I urge you not to use teabags – instead, loose-leaf Oolong will give you the most accurate flavour. With a full belly and a happy heart I left, with promises to meet Roohi and her team again.

I headed out early the next morning to taste the day's first *harissa*, which I had heard much about. In the winter months, early morning *harissa* is very much a ritual of the Kashmir valley. So, we headed to old Srinagar to taste another version of this rich, creamy mash, similar to the Hyderabadi *haleem* and the Persian *dizi*. Knowing I would be unable to finish such a rich and hearty dish so early in the morning, I shared – and the warming, filling *harissa* kept me going for hours.

HARISSA

LAMB HARISSA

SERVES 10–12

Harissa is better with lamb, but it can be made with chicken, too. Traditionally, the harissa is cooked overnight and served up at family brunches – it's a staple of many Kashmiri households. I've cut down the cooking time here, but the result is just as delicious. Sheekh Kebabs (page 34) are served as a garnish.

Pour sunflower oil into a deep, heavy-based pan to a depth of 8 cm (3 in). Place over a medium heat and heat to 180°C/350°F on a digital thermometer. Alternatively, you can drop in a tiny piece of bread: if it sizzles and browns in 15 seconds, the oil is hot enough.

Once the oil is hot, carefully add the shallots to the pan and deep-fry until crispy and brown. Remove with a slotted spoon and set aside to drain on a plate lined with paper towels.

Place the lamb leg in a large pan. Add the measured water and cook over a low heat for 3–4 hours, or until the meat falls away from the bone. Skim off and discard any scum that rises to the surface. When the broth is clear, add the garlic cloves, salt, ground ginger and all of the whole spices.

When the meat is cooked, remove from the heat and strain the cooking stock into a jug, discarding the whole spices. Remove the flesh from the bones and set the meat aside to rest.

Add the rice flour to the stock and whisk to combine, then place it back in the pan over a low heat. Add the milk and the cooked meat, and cook for at least 1 hour, stirring frequently, until the gravy is smooth.

Leave to rest before eating. When ready to eat, divide among bowls. Heat the ghee and pour it over the harissa, then serve garnished with sheekh kebabs and the crispy fried shallots.

INGREDIENTS

SUNFLOWER OIL, FOR DEEP-FRYING

500 G (1 LB 2 OZ) SHALLOTS, THINLY SLICED

1 KG (2 LB 4 OZ) LEG OF LAMB

2.5 LITRES (87 FL OZ/10 CUPS) WATER

12 GARLIC CLOVES, PEELED

1½ TEASPOONS SALT

2 TEASPOONS GROUND GINGER

1 TABLESPOON FENNEL SEEDS

6 WHOLE CLOVES

8 CM (3 IN) CINNAMON STICK

10 GREEN CARDAMOM PODS

6 BLACK CARDAMOM PODS

6 BLACK PEPPERCORNS

75 G (2½ OZ/GENEROUS ⅓ CUP) RICE FLOUR

250 ML (8½ FL OZ/1 CUP) MILK

4 TEASPOONS GHEE, TO SERVE

SHEEKH KEBABS (PAGE 34), TO SERVE

KOKUR YAKHNI

CHICKEN COOKED IN A YOGHURT AND
SAFFRON GRAVY

SERVES 6

This recipe is a labour of love. My dad's colleague used to cook it for us whenever there were celebrations. It requires patience, but the result is just superb. The chicken is boiled in milk, which makes it tender, and the warmth of the spices, yoghurt and saffron make it deliciously flavourful.

Place the chicken pieces in a large pan with the measured water and ½ teaspoon of the salt. Bring to the boil and simmer for 30 minutes until the meat is half cooked. Remove any scum that rises to the surface. Drain the chicken pieces and set aside.

Heat the ghee in a separate large pan with a lid over a high heat. Add the bay leaves and whole spices and fry for 1 minute, then add the garlic paste, shallot paste, ver masala, turmeric, ginger and the remaining 1 teaspoon of salt. Stir well, then add the chicken pieces. Stir to combine and cook for 4–5 minutes. Reduce the heat to low, add the whisked yoghurt and saffron milk, gently whisking so the yoghurt doesn't curdle. Cover and cook for 15 minutes, until the chicken is cooked through.

Serve hot with freshly cooked rice.

INGREDIENTS

1 X 1.5 KG (3 LB 5 OZ) WHOLE CHICKEN, SKIN REMOVED, CUT INTO PIECES

500 ML (17 FL OZ/2 CUPS) WATER

1½ TEASPOONS SALT

4 TEASPOONS GHEE

3 DRIED BAY LEAVES

8 CM (3 IN) CINNAMON STICK

4 WHOLE CLOVES, CRUSHED

6 GREEN CARDAMOM PODS

2 BLACK CARDAMOM PODS

10 G (½ OZ) GARLIC, CRUSHED TO A PASTE

2 TEASPOONS SHALLOT PASTE (PAGE 17)

2 TEASPOONS VER MASALA (PAGE 18)

1 TEASPOON GROUND TURMERIC

1 TEASPOON GROUND GINGER

200 G (7 OZ/GENEROUS ¾ CUP) GREEK YOGHURT, WHISKED

½ TEASPOON SAFFRON STRANDS, SOAKED IN 100 ML (3½ FL OZ/SCANT ½ CUP) LUKEWARM FULL-FAT MILK

STEAMED RICE, TO SERVE

SRINAGAR – THE LAND OF LAKES & GARDENS

One of the most scenic cities in Kashmir has to be Srinagar – it truly deserves its title of 'the land of lakes and gardens'. India's northernmost city, sitting 5,200 feet above sea level, it is home to a huge number of gardens dating back to the Mughal era, which all offer their own unique beauty throughout every season of the year. Many have one common element: a focus on symmetry, with beautiful geometric patterns dividing up these green spaces and giving them an inimitable style.

I couldn't have had a better tour guide than my driver, whose knowledge of Kashmir's history was incredible. He introduced me first to Shalimar Bagh, an impressive royal garden with tall chinar trees, beautiful flowers, a peaceful canal and *chini khanas*: arched niches behind waterfalls, that were, in the past, lit with oil lamps for an incredible visual effect. We also explored the Nishat Bagh Mughal garden, meaning 'garden of joy', and was designed by Asaf Khan, the elder brother of Nur Jahan. Its 12 terraces equate to the number of signs of the zodiac, and its fountains and central rectangular pool give the garden a feeling of true serenity. The view of the Dal Lake alone is both beautiful and hypnotising.

Next we visted the Tulip Garden, which was breathtaking. The largest tulip garden in the whole of Asia, spanning a 30-hectare area, it opened in 2007 with the aim of increasing tourism within the Kashmir Valley. Not only is the garden itself beautiful, but its setting too, sitting as it does among the foothills of the Zabarwan sub-mountain range, overlooking the Dal Lake. The most popular time of year to visit is in the spring, when the annual Tulip Festival takes place and the flowers are in full bloom. Visitors flock from all over India and beyond to marvel at the incredible fifty-plus varieties of tulip nurtured within the garden.

A guided tour meant that I could learn more about the place and its symbolism than I ever would have done alone. I hadn't realised that the tulip was the national flower of Turkey: long ago, the flower grew wild in Central Asia, and was cultivated in Turkey from the second century. In the 16th century, it was imported by Holland, where it is better known as a national flower.

One of the beautiful things about Srinagar is how easy it is to escape to nature when needed. In the foothills of Hari Parbat, the peak overlooking the city, you'll find Badamwari: the famous almond garden. It was lovely to see and hear families having picnics and the kids running around enjoying their freedom. The gardens themselves are well-maintained and incredibly beautiful – and are an incredible sight in the spring, when the swathes of almond trees bloom with their tiny white flowers. Here, you'll also find cherry trees, peach trees, tulip gardens and more. Every year, Badamwari hosts a popular festival where folk singers spread out across the gardens to entertain visitors.

Other must-sees on your trip include the well, built by Waris Khan during Akbar's reign, known as the Waris Khan Chah, as well as the open amphitheatre, where live concerts are organised in the spring. There are plenty of places where you can sit and admire the views, from the garden itself to Hari Parbat on one side, and Nageen Lake on the other.

GAAD

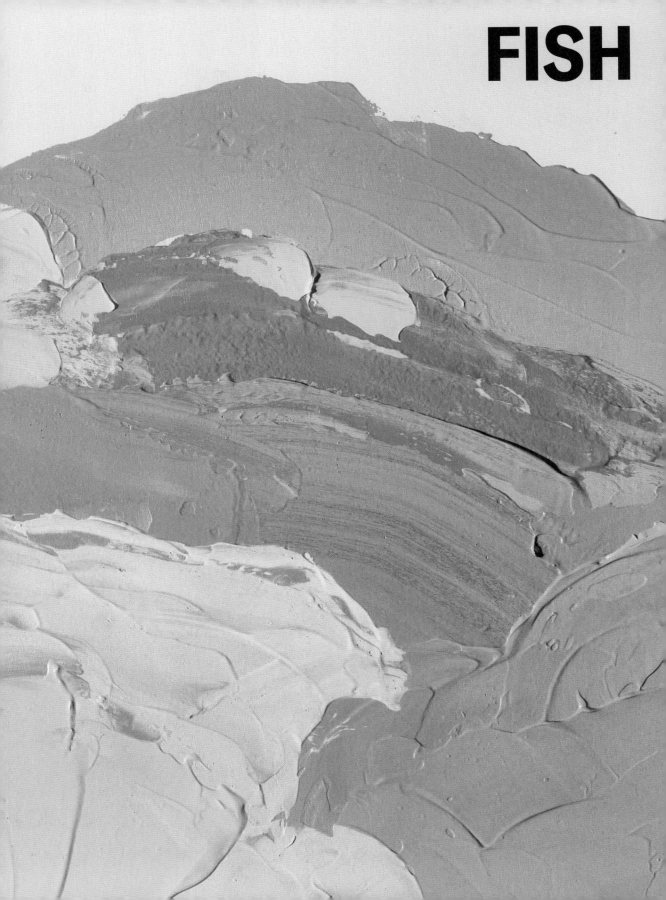

FISH

Kashmir is known for its harsh winters, when it can be hard to grow much food. For that reason, Kashmiri people often preserve foods to be enjoyed throughout the winter. One of these is the traditional smoked fish, known locally as *phari* or *pari*. The fish are caught in the region's numerous bountiful water, and hundreds are laid out on the dry grass beside the lakes. The locals set fire to the grass to smoke the fish, before leaving them to dry in the sun. They are then taken to be sold at local markets. For many people, it is a great source of income throughout the bitterly cold winter.

There are many ways to enjoy this smoked fish, but the most popular are to serve it with dried vegetables, in a tomato gravy, or with Kashmiri greens.

FRIED TROUT

WHOLE FRIED TROUT WITH SPICY
POTATO CHIPS

SERVES 2–3

On my last trip to Pahalgam, I had the most delicious fried trout ever. It was served on a trami, *a traditional arrangement consisting of various dishes served on a platter. The trout is marinated in spices and then deep-fried. I am using a whole trout, but typically the fish is cut into pieces. Serve with spicy chips for a Kashmiri take on fish and chips.*

Start with the fish. In a bowl, combine the garlic paste, rice flour, spices, lemon juice and salt, and mix to a paste. Pat the fish dry with paper towels and use a sharp knife to make several slits in the skin on top of each fish. Rub the fish all over with the spice paste and leave to marinate for 30 minutes at room temperature.

Pour the oil into a deep, heavy-based pan to a depth of 8 cm (3 in). Place over a medium heat and heat to 180°C/350°F on a digital thermometer. Alternatively, you can drop in a tiny piece of bread: if it sizzles and browns in 15 seconds, the oil is hot enough.

Once the oil is hot, fry the fish until they are both cooked through and the skin is crispy, about 5–7 minutes on each side. Remove from the pan and set aside to drain on a plate lined with paper towels. Bring the oil back to temperature.

For the spicy chips (fries), wash the potato chips under cold running water, then pat dry with paper towels. Place in a bowl, then add the chilli powder, turmeric and salt and toss until they are all well coated. Deep-fry until crispy, about 8 minutes, then remove to drain on paper towels.

Serve the fish and chips hot, with lemon wedges for squeezing over.

FOR THE FISH

4 LARGE GARLIC CLOVES CRUSHED TO A PASTE

1 TABLESPOON RICE FLOUR

2 TEASPOONS GROUND FENNEL

1 TEASPOON GREEN CARDAMOM SEEDS, FINELY CRUSHED

1 TEASPOON GROUND GINGER

1 TEASPOON GROUND TURMERIC

1 TEASPOON KASHMIRI CHILLI POWDER

½ TEASPOON GROUND CINNAMON

1 TABLESPOON FRESHLY SQUEEZED LEMON JUICE

1 TEASPOON SALT

2 WHOLE TROUT (APPROX. 550 G/1 LB 3 OZ), GUTTED, DESCALED AND WASHED

RAPESEED (CANOLA) OIL, FOR DEEP-FRYING

LEMON WEDGES, TO SERVE

FOR THE SPICY CHIPS (FRIES)

150 G (5 OZ) POTATOES, PEELED AND CUT INTO THICK FINGERS, THEN WASHED AND DRIED

½ TEASPOON KASHMIRI CHILLI POWDER

½ TEASPOON GROUND TURMERIC

1 TEASPOON SALT

RAPESEED (CANOLA) OIL, FOR DEEP-FRYING

GAAD TE TAMATAR

FISH IN TOMATO GRAVY

SERVES 4

Trout is usually used for this dish in Kashmir, but you can use any firm, white, meaty fish, such as hake or cod, or even salmon. This recipe is so delicious and very popular for special occasions.

Place the fish pieces in a bowl and add ½ teaspoon each of the salt and ground turmeric. Toss to coat, then leave to marinate for 20 minutes at room temperature.

Heat the oil in a sauté pan over a medium heat until very hot (if you are using mustard oil, ensure it is smoking hot before adding the fish). Fry the marinated fish for 3–4 minutes until lightly browned on all sides, then use a slotted spoon to remove the fish to a plate and set aside.

To the same pan, add the asafoetida and cook for 30 seconds, then add the chopped tomatoes and cook, still over a medium heat, for 5–6 minutes until soft. Add the rest of the spices along with the remaining ½ teaspoon each of salt and ground turmeric and cook for 1 minute, then add the hot water and bring to the boil. Reduce the heat to low, add the fried fish pieces and cook for a further 8–10 minutes until the gravy has thickened.

Serve with steamed rice.

INGREDIENTS

1 KG (2 LB 4 OZ) FISH (SEE INTRODUCTION), DESCALED, CLEANED AND CUT INTO 5 CM (2 IN) THICK PIECES

1 TEASPOON SALT

1 TEASPOON GROUND TURMERIC

3½ TABLESPOONS RAPESEED (CANOLA) OIL OR MUSTARD OIL

1 TEASPOON ASAFOETIDA POWDER

250 G (9 OZ) TOMATOES, CHOPPED

1–2 TEASPOONS KASHMIRI CHILLI POWDER

2 TEASPOONS GROUND GINGER

1 TEASPOON VER MASALA (PAGE 18)

250 ML (8½ FL OZ/1 CUP) HOT WATER

STEAMED RICE, TO SERVE

MUJI GAAD

SEA BASS WITH TURNIPS

SERVES 2

Whole sea bass, marinated, fried and served with a delicious cooked turnip sauce. If you don't like preparing whole fish, use a fish that is already prepped and sliced. You can use sea bream or trout for this dish, too.

Place the fish in a wide, shallow bowl and sprinkle with ½ teaspoon of the salt, ½ teaspoon of the ground turmeric and the lemon juice. Set aside to marinate at room temperature for 20 minutes.

Heat 1 tablespoon of the oil in a sauté pan over a medium heat until very hot (if you are using mustard oil, ensure it is smoking hot before adding the fish). Fry the marinated fish for 3 minutes on each side until crispy, then use a slotted spoon to remove the fish to a plate and set aside. Alternatively, sprinkle the fish with 1 tablespoon of the oil and grill (broil) for 7–8 minutes under a hot grill (broiler) until crispy.

Heat the remaining tablespoon of oil in a pan over a medium–high heat, then fry the turnips until golden. Remove the turnips to a separate plate.

To the same pan, add the garlic paste, chilli paste, shallot paste, ver masala, ground ginger and fennel, and the remaining 1 teaspoon salt and ½ teaspoon turmeric. Mix well and cook over a medium heat for 1 minute. Add the hot water and bring to the boil, then let it simmer for 3–4 minutes before returning the fried turnips to the pan. Cook until the gravy has thickened, then remove from the heat.

To serve, place the whole fish onto a platter and pour over the turnip gravy. Serve with steamed rice.

INGREDIENTS

1 X 500 G (1 LB 2 OZ) WHOLE SEA BASS, GUTTED, DESCALED AND WASHED

1½ TEASPOONS SALT

1 TEASPOON GROUND TURMERIC

JUICE OF ½ LEMON

2 TABLESPOONS RAPESEED (CANOLA) OIL OR MUSTARD OIL

500 G (1 LB 2 OZ) TURNIPS, PEELED AND DICED INTO CHUNKS

4 LARGE GARLIC CLOVES, CRUSHED TO A PASTE

2 TEASPOONS KASHMIRI CHILLI PASTE

2 TEASPOONS SHALLOT PASTE (PAGE 17)

2 TEASPOONS VER MASALA (PAGE 18)

2 TEASPOONS GROUND GINGER

1 TEASPOON GROUND FENNEL

200 ML (7 FL OZ/SCANT 1 CUP) HOT WATER

STEAMED RICE, TO SERVE

GAAD TE HAAKH

FISH COOKED WITH SPINACH

SERVES 2

Spinach forms a part of various dishes in Kashmir, as it combines so well with other ingredients. I have eaten spinach with paneer, chicken and lamb, but never with fish, so this dish was a first for me. I have used haddock but any firm fish works really well, here.

Place the fish in a wide, shallow bowl and sprinkle with ½ teaspoon of the ground turmeric and a pinch of salt. Set aside to marinate at room temperature for 20 minutes.

Place the spinach in a large saucepan, along with the black cardamom pods, ½ teaspoon each of the turmeric and salt, and the measured hot water. Bring to the boil and cook for 4 minutes until the spinach is tender. Do not drain.

Heat the oil in a separate frying pan (skillet) over a medium heat, then fry the fish for 2–3 minutes on each side until browned. Remove from the pan and set aside on a plate. To the same pan, add the shallots and cook for 5–6 minutes, then add the ver masala, garlic and chilli powder, along with the remaining ½ teaspoon of salt. Place the fish gently back into the pan, without breaking the fish. Add the spinach, along with its cooking water, and cook for a final 3–4 minutes.

Serve with rice.

INGREDIENTS

2 HADDOCK FILLETS (APPROX. 500 G/1 LB 2 OZ)

1 TEASPOON GROUND TURMERIC

1 TEASPOON SALT, PLUS A PINCH

500 G (1 LB 2 OZ) SPINACH, WASHED

2 BLACK CARDAMOM PODS

300 ML (10 FL OZ/1¼ CUPS) HOT WATER

2 TABLESPOONS MUSTARD OIL OR RAPESEED (CANOLA) OIL

100 G (3½ OZ) SHALLOTS, SLICED

1 TEASPOON VER MASALA (PAGE 18)

6 GARLIC CLOVES, CRUSHED TO A PASTE

1–2 TEASPOONS KASHMIRI CHILLI POWDER

STEAMED RICE, TO SERVE

GAAD CHOONTH

FISH COOKED WITH QUINCE
OR GREEN APPLES

SERVES 2–3

The delicate trout balances the spices in this recipe, and the tangy sweetness of quince works like magic with the fish. If you can't find quince, use delicious green apples instead. You can also cook this recipe with radishes. I love eating this on its own, but you can serve it with rice.

Place the fish pieces in a bowl and add ½ teaspoon each of the salt and ground turmeric. Toss to coat, then leave to marinate for 15 minutes at room temperature.

Heat the oil in a sauté pan over a medium heat until very hot (if you are using mustard oil, ensure it is smoking hot before adding the fish).

Fry the marinated fish until crispy on all sides, then use a slotted spoon to transfer it to a plate. Set aside.

To the same pan over a medium heat, add the asafoetida and all the spices, including the remaining ½ teaspoon of turmeric, and cook for 30 seconds, then add the quince or apples and cook for 8–10 minutes until golden. Add the remaining ½ teaspoon of salt, along with the sugar, chilli paste and water, and cook for 5 minutes, then add the cooked fish and cook for a further 2–3 minutes before serving.

INGREDIENTS

1 X 750 G (1 LB 10 OZ) WHOLE TROUT, GUTTED, DESCALED, WASHED AND CUT INTO FILLETS

1 TEASPOON SALT

1 TEASPOON GROUND TURMERIC

4 TEASPOONS MUSTARD OIL OR RAPESEED (CANOLA) OIL

½ TEASPOON ASAFOETIDA POWDER

2 TEASPOONS GROUND FENNEL

2 TEASPOONS GROUND GINGER

1 TEASPOON GROUND CLOVES

½ TEASPOON FRESHLY GROUND BLACK PEPPER

500 G (1 LB 2 OZ) QUINCE OR GREEN EATING APPLES, EACH SLICED INTO 4 PIECES

1 TEASPOON BROWN SUGAR

2 TEASPOONS KASHMIRI CHILLI PASTE

200 ML (7 FL OZ/SCANT 1 CUP) HOT WATER

RESOURCEFULNESS AT WULAR LAKE

It was through Instagram that I first met two Kashmiri food bloggers who were keen to show me their local area through their eyes. The first, Umar, told me that, as he didn't have a sister, he had grown up helping his mother in the kitchen, which gave him the confidence and knowledge he needed to be able to cook for himself. From there, he started his Instagram account – @kashmirfoodgram – where he began to explore delicacies from across Kashmir. Later, he realised that he should also be covering the region's seasonal culinary treats, and he has developed a true love of and curiosity about food that has led him to many unexplored places, and many exciting dishes.

Like me, Umar is keen to share the joys of Kashmiri cuisine with the world. When he learned that I was in Srinagar, he contacted me, arranging a day with himself and fellow food blogger, Muhammed. Muhammed's food blogging journey began in 2017, and his aim was to show that Kashmiri food isn't just about the *wazwan*, but that it's an incredibly diverse cuisine with plenty to offer. Through his blog – Kashmirfoods – he's become one of the biggest social media names in Kashmir, sharing all sorts of food events and restaurants, from glitzy cafes to delicious street food, to showcase Kashmiri food and culture.

Umar and Muhammed were keen to show me the Wular Lake which is the livelihood of thousands of fishermen in the area (I was not able to go with them, but went with my sister in law later). Located between the towns of Sopur and Bandippore, it's the second-largest freshwater lake in Asia – 10 km (over 6 miles) wide and nearly 24 km (15 miles) long. According to Hindu mythology, this natural flood reservoir, which drains excess water from the Jhelum River, is said to be the remains of the Satisar Lake – the lake of the Goddess Sati – which stood in the region in prehistoric times. I was smitten by its beauty – bounded on all sides by snow-clad hills, it was undoubtedly one of the highlights of my trip.

Umar and Muhammed explained to me just how important the lake is to Kashmir, for so many reasons. We spent some time simply watching the myriad varieties of fish making their way through the water, and I learned that Wular Lake alone is responsible for around 60 per cent of

Kashmir's entire fish yield, and that around 10,000 fishermen flock to this lake to make a living.

The fish aren't the only food source that Wular provides, said Umar. He described how local farmers rely on the lake's bountiful supply of water chestnuts during the winter: collecting them from the marshy water, then cleaning them before laying them out in the sun to dry. When they turn white, he explained, they are ready to sell in the market, and they are popular with Kashmiri people, who eat them raw, roasted, boiled or fried during the harsh winter months.

The humble water chestnut gave me a great insight into how resourceful and resilient the Kashmiri people are. When floods devastated Kashmir and decimated crop fields, says Umar, people ground water chestnuts into flour to save themselves from starvation.

It was fascinating to meet Umar and Muhammed, and to learn more about the region and how its people source their food, from two people who are clearly incredibly passionate and knowledgable about their region's food history and culture. I'm looking forward to my next trip, when they have promised to introduce me to their favourite delicacies in Srinagar's old city.

GAAD FRY

FRIED WHITEBAIT OR SARDINES

SERVES 4

My journey to the Hazaratbal Shrine led to the Foreshore Road in Hazratbal, where I tasted the fried whitebait. I loved it so much that I had it at Dal Lake in Srinagar, too!

To make the batter, combine the rice flour, spices, salt and water in a large bowl and whisk to a smooth paste. Once the batter is smooth, add the fish and mix together. Set aside.

Pour the oil into a deep, heavy-based pan to a depth of 8 cm (3 in). Place over a medium heat and heat to 180°C/350°F on a digital thermometer. Alternatively, you can drop in a tiny piece of the batter: if it floats up to the surface and sizzles and browns in 15 seconds, the oil is hot enough. Once the oil is hot, carefully add the spice-coated fish and fry until evenly cooked and crispy, about 5 minutes. Remove with a slotted spoon to drain on paper towels. You may need to do this in batches.

Enjoy with chutney or tomato ketchup, and serve with lemon wedges on the side for squeezing.

INGREDIENTS

75 G (2½ OZ/GENEROUS ⅓ CUP) RICE FLOUR, SIFTED

1–2 TEASPOONS KASHMIRI CHILLI POWDER

1 TEASPOON GROUND CUMIN

1 TEASPOON GROUND TURMERIC

1 TEASPOON FRESHLY GROUND BLACK PEPPER

1 TEASPOON GROUND GINGER

1 TEASPOON GROUND FENNEL

1 TEASPOON SALT

100 ML (3½ FL OZ/SCANT ½ CUP) WATER

12 WHITEBAIT OR SARDINES

SUNFLOWER OIL, FOR DEEP-FRYING

TO SERVE

CHUTNEY OR TOMATO KETCHUP

LEMON WEDGES

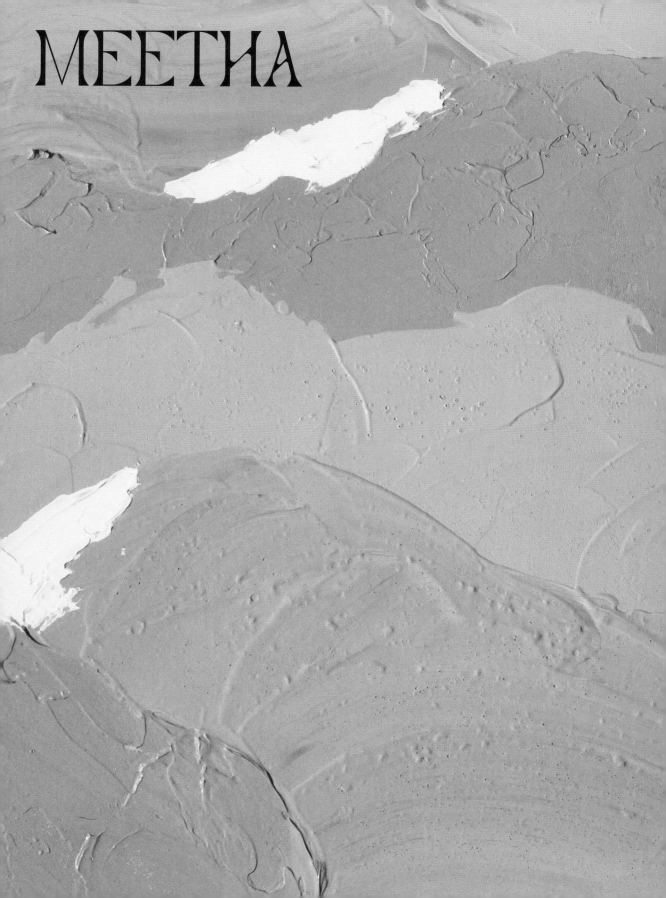

MEETHA

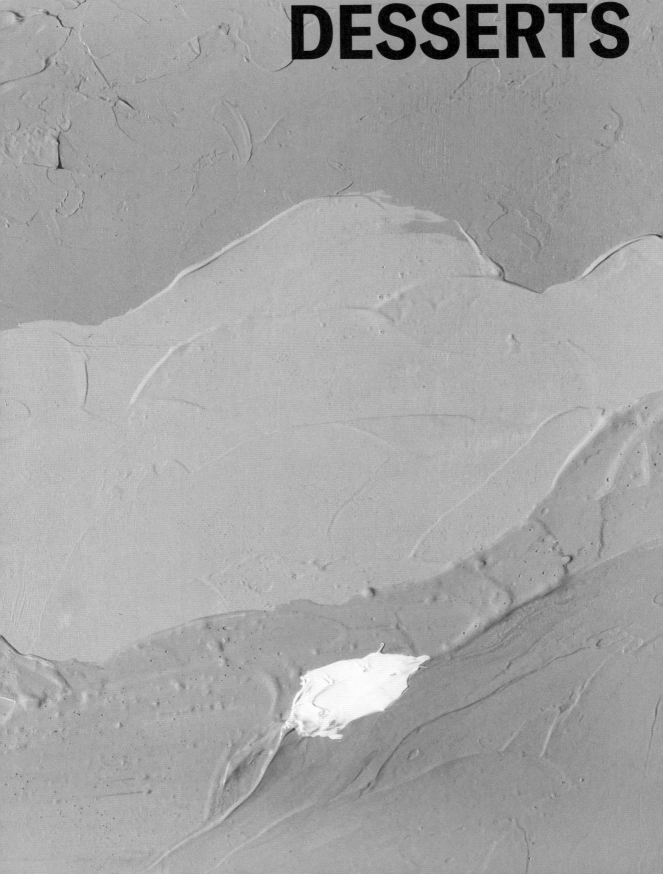

DESSERTS

In India, it's certainly common to have a sweet tooth. Wherever there is a celebration, or after a meal, sweets are present. During my time in Kashmir, I saw the importance of bakery culture in the region, and discovered just how important a role cakes and pastries play in every day life. This is partly because of the rich crossover of cultures there: the traditional recipes from different backgrounds still exist and are much loved by all.

KONG PHIRNI

SAFFRON-FLAVOURED SEMOLINA

SERVES 6–8

Kong Phirni is a creamy dessert that is a great way to finish your meal. While the traditional phirni in northern India is made with ground rice, in Kashmir it is made with suji (semolina) flavoured with saffron. I had this phirni at Wafa's place. It was so delicious, and so I wanted the recipe to be part of this book.

Pour the milk into a deep saucepan. Add the saffron and bring to the boil over a medium heat. Add the semolina to the hot milk and stir continuously for about 15 minutes until the mixture thickens to the consistency of gravy.

Add the sugar and condensed milk and cook for a further 5 minutes, then remove from the heat and leave to cool.

Pour into ramikins and sprinkle with the cashew and pistachio nuts before serving.

INGREDIENTS

1 LITRE (34 FL OZ/4 CUPS) FULL-FAT (WHOLE) MILK

10 SAFFRON STRANDS

50 G (2 OZ/SCANT ½ CUP) FINE SEMOLINA

100 G (3½ OZ/SCANT ½ CUP) CASTER (SUPERFINE) SUGAR

100 G (3½ OZ/⅓ CUP) CONDENSED MILK

15 G (½ OZ/1½ TABLESPOONS) CASHEW NUTS, CHOPPED

15 G (½ OZ/1½ TABLESPOONS) PISTACHIOS, CHOPPED

SHAKER PARE

SWEET DEEP-FRIED SNACKS

SERVES 6–8

Amit and I were having a conversation about chestnut flour, and he told me about these lovely chestnut-flour snacks they eat and make for ceremonies. Chestnut flour needs to be treated with care, but they are worth the effort they require. They can be stored in an airtight container and enjoyed any time.

Place the sugar and water in a pan and bring to the boil until the sugar has dissolved. Remove from the heat and cool to room temperature.

In a bowl, combine the flour, crushed fennel seeds and measured oil or ghee and bring together, making sure there are no loose crumbs, before gently adding the sugar water. Knead into a dough, then leave to rest for 10 minutes.

Pour sunflower oil into a deep, heavy-based pan to a depth of 8 cm (3 in). Place over a medium heat and heat to 180°C/350°F on a digital thermometer. Alternatively, you can drop in a tiny piece of bread: if it sizzles and browns in 15 seconds, the oil is hot enough.

While the oil is getting hot, divide the dough into 4 equal-sized balls, dust with a little flour and roll out as you would a chapatti. Cut each disc into 5 cm (2 in) diamond-shaped pieces.

Once the oil is hot, fry the diamonds for 3–4 minutes until brown and crispy. You may need to do this in batches. Remove to drain on paper towels.

Store in an airtight container for 2–3 weeks and enjoy with a cup of chai or on their own.

INGREDIENTS

200 G (7 OZ/GENEROUS 1 CUP) BROWN SUGAR

275 ML (9 FL OZ/GENEROUS 1 CUP) WATER, AT ROOM TEMPERATURE

350 G (12 OZ/2⅓ CUPS) CHESTNUT FLOUR, PLUS EXTRA FOR DUSTING

2 TEASPOONS FENNEL SEEDS, CRUSHED

100 ML (3½ FL OZ/SCANT ½ CUP) SUNFLOWER OIL OR GHEE

SUNFLOWER OIL, FOR DEEP-FRYING

EXPLORING THE ARU & BETAAB VALLEYS

I decided I should make the effort to visit Pahalgam: a hill station 95 km (60 miles) from Srinagar, known as the 'Valley of Shepherds'. Surrounded by towering pine forests, beautiful meadows and the lofty snow-capped Himalayan mountains, Pahalgam has long been a popular location for Bollywood film shoots. With my hotel booked, I set off with my driver, Bhuran. I was mentally and physically drained as a result of the change in time zone, but my excitement overtook my tiredness. Even Bhuran – normally of very few words – was excitedly chattering to me about all the places I should visit.

As it turned out, Bhuran couldn't show me these sights himself – all journeys must be taken by local taxi, which was arranged through the hotel. Our first stop was the Aru Valley. It's the base camp for those who come here to trek to the Kolhoi Glacier and Tarsar-Masar lake, and is a fantastic place for outdoor activities of all kinds: horse riding, hiking, trekking – even skiing during the winter months, when the snow comes tumbling down.

The sights I saw on the drive through the Aru Valley evoked all sorts of emotions and memories. Seeing people picnicking by the banks of the river reminded me of childhood excursions with friends, and seeing the Gujjar families and their clay-built houses filled me with intrigue. I asked my driver if it was possible for us to stop so I could visit the families: it turned out to be one of the best decisions of my trip.

I stood a while and smiled as I watched the Gujjar children playing, and when a young man appeared, I asked if it was possible for me to take a look inside their home. He agreed. Throughout my whole trip the Kashmiri people were kind and welcoming, but this was a whole new experience. I was impressed with the beauty of their home: the inside so well-kept, the walls adorned with beautiful drawings. The small *chulah* – a traditional open stove crafted from clay – was a focal point, and their home also featured a hot water tank, with the water warmed by the heat of the fire when it was lit for cooking. I was astounded by the cleverness of their self-sufficiency. After tea and roti, I left with promises that we would cook for each other on my return. The promise to meet again is what I always look forward to – and already I can't wait to go back.

From there, we set off to the Betaab Valley, which was given its name after the popular 1983 movie *Betaab*.

Lying between two Himalayan ranges – Pir Panzal and Zanskar – the Betaab Valleys came under the rule of the Mughals in the fifteenth century, when it was known as the Hagoon Valley. It sits between Pahalgam and Chandanwadi – a popular route to the famous Amarnath Temple – and is also a base camp for the Amarnath Yatra, a popular Hindu pilgrimage. The temple is known as one of Hinduism's holiest shrines, and lies within a snow-covered cave surrounded by mountains, with access possible for just a few summer weeks each year.

Pahalgam isn't just a pilgrimage site – far from it. Its two-day Snow Festival, which takes place in either January or February each year, showcases the town's winter adventure sports, as well as artwork, traditional crafts, music and dance performances. Golf is another major draw of the area, as well as rafting through the forests and down the rapids of the Lidder River. Both tourism and film-making almost came to a halt, with the threat of militancy hanging over the valley for over 30 years, but now, the situation appears to be improving.

If you do visit, I would recommend buying Kashmiri shawls, carpets or chain-stitched embroidered clothing as souvenirs – they are true works of art. And from souvenir shopping to tour guides, I would urge visitors to please not barter with the locals. The tourism industry has already suffered many terrible years, and those tourists who do visit can play their part in rebuilding this incredible town.

On my second trip to the area, I woke and left early to visit Pahalgam. While it was a chilly start to the morning, the sun eventually peeped through the clouds, casting a beautiful light across the yellow mustard fields that we passed by. We drove through the municipality of Aishmuquam in Anantnag district, where we saw kids clasping local flatbreads in their hands. Intrigued, we stopped to find out more, and they pointed us in the direction of the local bakery. In a tiny room with a tandoor oven, we found a lovely lady rolling piece after piece of *bakarkhani*. These flatbreads resemble naan, but are prepared more like roti, stretched, kneaded and layered with sesame seeds, and sometimes flavoured with rose water, raisins or cardamom. The baker let us stop and watch a while, explaining that these breads are typically eaten warm at breakfast, often with a steaming cup of *noon chai*.

Fresh, hot bread bought, we continued through idyllic scenery: a parade of sheep approaching the road with *bakarwal* (shepherds) urging them on; the sparkling Lidder River in the distance; young shepherds' kids sitting by the river with the horses, chatting amongst themselves. It wasn't sheep that awaited me in Pahalgam, but cows – or rather, their produce. Amit had arranged a meeting with Dutch-born Chris Zandee, who founded Himalayan Products in 2007. Since then, he has become renowned for his artisan cheese, with a commitment to social and responsible sourcing and production, and to following international standards. It was incredible to see a foreigner supporting this tight-knit local community in so many ways, from sourcing milk from semi-nomadic Gujjar dairy farmers to creating local jobs in his small factory

CONTINUED ON PAGE 162

in Langanbal village. Together with Amna Gorshi and Shabbir Ahmed, two members of his team, Chris first showed me their traditional Gujjar cheese, known as *kalari* or *maish krej* – a dense and stretchy cheese that has a similar mildness to mozzarella.

My tasting session soon moved on to cheeses with more international influence. Inspired by his Dutch roots, Chris also produces Gouda: mild and almost sweet when young, nuttier and more buttery as it ages. He had also specialised in different Gouda flavours to suit both traditional and more adventurous palates, including cumin, fenugreek and walnut, all of which he has mastered incredibly well. His Cheddar is also popular and, like the others, is sold all over India. It's not just the local milk that Chris and his team use, but also fruits that are grown across the Kashmir region. These are picked, prepared and cooked to create a range of jams, with flavours including mulberry, cherry, peach and more.

Chris's colleague Shabbir had kindly extended an invitation to us to dine at his house, alongside his wife and children. It was the most incredible vegetarian lunch of cornmeal roti and *saag*, made with greens they had picked from the wild, all washed down with *noon chai*.

Fully satiated, Shabbir's sister Reshma took us to the Pahalgam Hotel, which was established back in 1931 by the great grandfather of Kashmiri Sikh, Ramneek Kaur, who now runs the establishment with her family. Within the hotel, she has set up an incredible shop: a treasure trove of traditional Kashmiri crafts, such as embroidered shawls, wickerwork, papier mache crafts and more, all handmade by women like Reshma. All of this is possible through the Shepherdcrafts initiative, set up by Ramneek and Devika Krishnan in 2011. It's an initiative that serves multiple purposes. It seeks to both revive and sustain the incredible craftsmanship of the local Gujjar and Bakarwal shepherd tribes who are native to the region, documenting their processes, and selling their creations. It also provide these tribal women with a sustainable income, helping them to gain access to healthcare and education, which can be a challenge due to their nomadic lifestyle.

Ramneek is a useful person to know when it comes to exploring the lifestyles of the Gujjar and Bakarwal tribes. As well as Shepherdcrafts, she also organises a 'Shepherd's Trail', which takes you on the tribes' secrets paths through the forests, plus a 'Shepherd's Meal' at the Pahalgam Hotel, where you can feast on traditional tribal fare.

While travelling back to the city at the end of the day, my eyes were tired, but I was still mesmerised by the sights that flashed past the car windows: apple blossom in the small orchards; kids playing cricket in their *pherans* (traditional Kashmiri gowns). We stopped to take photos of the game, itself a language of team work, and I noticed a mother and her daughters handing out *tehar* – turmeric or yellow rice – to all of the other kids. When I asked the mother why, she replied that they were celebrating a birthday: this rice dish is synonymous with celebrations and religious occasions throughout Kashmir.

HALWA

SEMOLINA PUDDING WITH NUTS

SERVES 8

Halwa is enjoyed by many cultures across India, and is made with different ingredients all over the country. I was fed something very similar to this, with Phirni *(page 154), during my second trip to Kashmir. I love having it with a cup of chai.*

In a saucepan combine the water, sugar, crushed green cardamom seeds and saffron. Place over a medium heat and bring to the boil. Boil for 10 minutes, then remove from the heat.

Heat the ghee in a separate pan over a medium heat. Add the semolina and fry for around 10 minutes until brown. Slowly add the sugar water and mix thoroughly to a lovely, crumbly consistency, then stir in the chopped cashew nuts and raisins.

Just before serving, sprinkle with the toasted almond flakes.

INGREDIENTS

650 ML (22 FL OZ/2¾ CUPS) WATER

150 G (5 OZ/⅔ CUP) CASTER (SUPERFINE) SUGAR

SEEDS FROM 4 GREEN CARDAMOM PODS, CRUSHED

½ TEASPOON SAFFRON STRANDS

100 G (3½ OZ) GHEE

200 G (7 OZ/GENEROUS 1½ CUPS) COARSE SEMOLINA

20 G (¾ OZ/2 TABLESPOONS) CASHEW NUTS, CHOPPED

20 G (¾ OZ/2½ TABLESPOONS) RAISINS

4 TEASPOONS TOASTED FLAKED (SLIVERED) ALMONDS

ROOH AFZA

ROSE SYRUP DRINK

MAKES 2

Anyone growing up in India will remember this. A bright, rose-flavoured syrup made up with milk, soda water and ice, or even just water, it makes a very cooling and refreshing summer drink.

The syrup was a regular in our house while I was growing up. I didn't like it initially, but eventually I fell in love with this sugary, refreshing drink. My friends and I used to eat crushed ice lollies with the syrup poured over them. We also used to visit a place in Kolkata to eat the falooda *pudding, which contained this syrup. It can be bought online and in Asian speciality stores.*

Add the *rooh afza* and sugar to the cold milk and soda water, and mix well. Serve over crushed ice, with extra syrup drizzled on top.

INGREDIENTS

60 ML (2 FL OZ/¼ CUP) ROOH AFZA SYRUP, PLUS EXTRA FOR DRIZZLING

4 TEASPOONS CASTER (SUPERFINE) SUGAR

500 ML (17 FL OZ/2 CUPS) COLD MILK

200 ML (7 FL OZ/SCANT 1 CUP) SODA WATER

CRUSHED ICE, TO SERVE

KAHWA

KASHMIRI SPICED HONEY TEA

SERVES 2

INGREDIENTS

600 ML (20 FL OZ/2½ CUPS) WATER

8 CM (3 IN) CINNAMON STICK

2 GREEN CARDAMOM PODS

2 WHOLE CLOVES

1 TEASPOON GROUND GINGER

1 TABLESPOON HONEY

2 BLACK PEPPERCORNS

½ TEASPOON GREEN TEA LEAVES

PINCH OF SAFFRON STRANDS, PLUS EXTRA TO DECORATE

6 BLANCHED ALMONDS, CHOPPED, TO DECORATE

Kahwa is a Kashmiri tea flavoured or infused with spices, saffron, honey and almonds. It is a great drink to enjoy throughout the year, but especially in winter.

Place all the ingredients, except the chopped almonds, in a pan and bring to the boil.

Strain into a teapot.

Serve the tea hot, garnished with a few saffron strands and the chopped almonds.

SHEER/NOON CHAI

PINK SALTY TEA

MAKES 2

INGREDIENTS

600 ML (20 FL OZ/2½ CUPS) WATER, OR MORE AS NEEDED

2 TEASPOONS GREEN TEA LEAVES

PINCH OF BICARBONATE OF SODA (BAKING SODA)

2 TEASPOONS CHOPPED ALMONDS

1 TEASPOON GREEN CARDAMOM SEEDS, CRUSHED

400 ML (13 FL OZ/GENEROUS 1½ CUPS) MILK

1 TEASPOON SALT

This pink tea is salty and sweet and so refreshing. The pink colour is created by the bicarbonate of soda (baking soda).

Bring the water to the boil in a pan with a lid, then add the tea leaves and the bicarbonate of soda. Cover and let it boil for 10–12 minutes. If the water starts drying up, add another 100 ml (3½ fl oz/scant ½ cup) water.

Add the chopped almonds and crushed green cardamom seeds, along with the milk, and bring back to the boil. Add the salt and serve immediately, or keep in a thermos flask to drink later.

BAITH, CHAUTT & CHETIN

BREADS, RICE & CHUTNEYS

Although the staple diet of the Kashmiris has to be rice – a meal is not considered complete without it – there are many other sides and accompaniments that add extra enjoyment to every dish. Across Kashmir, different breads are eaten at different times of the day, and the taste of freshly baked flatbreads with their *noon chai* or *kahwa* is so delicious.

Chutneys, relishes and pickles are a common way to make produce last longer so that it can be enjoyed when not in season. Pickles are easy to make, and the end result is superb, bringing joy to your meals. Relishes are delicious as part of meal, or as a lighter option if you just want something small. Wherever you eat in Kashmir, the sides are what makes the meals extra special.

BATHA

STEAMED/BOILED RICE

SERVES 4

INGREDIENTS

250 G (9 OZ/1¼ CUPS) BASMATI RICE

1 LITRE (34 FL OZ/4 CUPS) WATER

Rice is the staple food of Kashmiris. Batha is popular and it's easy to prepare. It goes well with all dishes.

Place the rice and water in a deep saucepan and bring to the boil over a high heat, then reduce to a simmer and cook for 10 minutes. Drain and enjoy with your meal.

TAHER

YELLOW RICE

SERVES 8–10

INGREDIENTS

500 G (1 LB 2 OZ/2½ CUPS) BASMATI RICE

2 TEASPOONS GROUND TURMERIC

1½ TEASPOONS SALT

4 TEASPOONS MUSTARD OIL OR RAPESEED (CANOLA) OIL

Taher *rice (pictured right) is cooked with turmeric and mixed with oil and salt, and is highly symbolic in Kashmiri culture. Both Kashmiri Pandits and Muslims cook it for birthdays or celebrations. My driver, Younis, said the only difference is Muslims add* praan *(shallots). It is also cooked for offering to the deities and distributing at shrines or among neighbours. Serve with pickles and yoghurt.*

Place the rice, ground turmeric and salt in a large pan and cover with water. Bring to the boil over a high heat, then reduce the heat and cook for 15 minutes until the rice is nearly cooked but still has a bite to it. Drain, cover the pan and leave to rest for 5 minutes.

Heat the oil in a separate pan, then pour it over the rice and mix it through.

MODUR PULAO

SAFFRON PILAU

SERVES 8–10

I love this recipe. Modur pulao *is a sweet pulao from Kashmir flavoured with saffron and combined with dried fruits, nuts and a good amount of ghee. My mum used to make similar recipe called* zarda*. I was so glad I was able to try this recipe during my visits. It is usually paired with spicy curries.*

Place the rice in a deep pan and cover with water. Bring to the boil, then reduce to a simmer and cook for 5 minutes until the rice is half cooked. Drain and set aside.

In a separate small pan, combine the measured water with the sugar, saffron and all the whole spices. Bring to the boil over a high heat and cook until the sugar has completely dissolved. Remove from the heat.

Heat the ghee in another large pan with a lid over a low heat. Add the dates, raisins, coconut and blanched almonds, and cook for 1 minute. Add the half-cooked rice and the sugar syrup, along with the whole spices. Bring to a simmer, then reduce the heat to low, cover and cook for 5–6 minutes before serving.

INGREDIENTS

500 G (1 LB 2 OZ/2½ CUPS) BASMATI RICE

300 ML (10 FL OZ/1¼ CUPS) WATER, PLUS EXTRA FOR COOKING THE RICE

100 G (3½ OZ/SCANT ½ CUP) GOLDEN CASTER (SUPERFINE) OR BROWN SUGAR

½ TEASPOON SAFFRON STRANDS

5 WHOLE CLOVES

8 CM (3 IN) CINNAMON STICK

4 GREEN CARDAMOM PODS

2 BLACK CARDAMOM PODS

50 G (2 OZ) GHEE

6 DRIED DATES, ROUGHLY CHOPPED

30 G (1 OZ/¼ CUP) RAISINS

15 G (½ OZ/¼ CUP) DRIED COCONUT CHUNKS (CHIPS)

30 G (1 OZ/¼ CUP) BLANCHED ALMONDS

BAITH, CHAUTT & CHETIN

MAKAI TCHOT

MAIZE FLOUR FLATBREAD

SERVES 4

The Bakarwal people rarely eat rice or wheat. What I love about this recipe is that you don't need to prove the dough. The traditional method is rather difficult and requires lots of practice – the dough can't be rolled out, as maize flour contains only a small amount of gluten and sticks a lot. For this reason, many people prefer to use the freezer bag or baking paper technique. Serve with Haakh *(page 47).*

Sift the flour into a bowl, then add a little hot water and knead with the heel of your hands. Very gradually add more water, kneading until you have a smooth dough.

Divide the dough into 4 portions, each about the size of a tennis ball. Place a ball of dough on top of a freezer bag or on a sheet of baking paper. Flatten it out with your fingers a little bit, then, with wet hands, pat the dough out to form a disc about 3 mm (⅛ in) thick.

Meanwhile, heat a frying pan (skillet) or griddle over a medium heat. Once the pan is hot, place the first flatbread gently in the pan and cook until small air bubbles form on the bottom, then flip and cook the other side. It takes 3–4 minutes to cook each side properly. Repeat with the remaining dough.

INGREDIENTS

200 G (7 OZ/GENEROUS 1½ CUPS) MAIZE (CORNMEAL) FLOUR

100 ML (3½ FL OZ/SCAN ½ CUP) BOILING WATER, BUT ADD MORE AS NEEDED, TO BIND THE DOUGH

KASHMIRI KANDER/GIRDA

NAAN OR FLATBREAD

MAKES 4–5

Kashmiris love to have freshly baked bread from the bakery. When I was in Kashmir, I got to visit many bakers in different villages and colonies known as the kandur. *Most of the breads are made in the* tandoor *oven before dawn so people can enjoy them in the morning with a cup of* noon chai *(salty pink tea, page 168).*

In a mixing bowl, combine the flour, sugar, salt and yeast, and mix them together. Gently add the lukewarm water and knead into a soft ball of dough. This will take about 8–10 minutes. Apply the melted ghee to the dough, turning it to coat, then leave to prove, covered, at room temperature for 1 hour.

Preheat the oven to 220°C (200°C fan/425°F/gas 7) and place an ovenproof frying pan (cast-iron skillet) in the oven to heat up.

Knock back and knead the risen dough for a minute or two, then divide into 4–5 equal-sized balls.

Lightly dust with flour. With wet hands, stretch each dough ball with your palm to about 3 mm (⅛ in) thick and 5 cm (2 in) in diameter. Gently press a pattern into the surface with your fingertips, then sprinkle with poppy seeds.

Place the first bread on the hot pan and cook in the oven for 1–2 minutes on each side. Repeat until all the breads are cooked.

INGREDIENTS

250 G (9 OZ/2 CUPS) PLAIN (ALL-PURPOSE) FLOUR, PLUS EXTRA FOR DUSTING

1 TEASPOON CASTER (SUPERFINE) SUGAR

½ TEASPOON SALT

6 G (2 TEASPOONS) FAST-ACTION DRIED YEAST

175–200 ML (6–7 FL OZ/¾–SCANT 1 CUP) LUKEWARM WATER, PLUS EXTRA AS NEEDED

2 TEASPOONS MELTED GHEE

2 TEASPOONS WHITE POPPY SEEDS

BAKARKHANI

SWEET PUFF PASTRY BISCUITS

MAKES 5–6

Bakarkhani is the gift of the Mughals to India, along with many other delicious dishes. Across India, bakarkhani keep changing in texture, size and shape. When I was in Kashmir, I got to taste a couple of different kinds: one made bakery-style with puff pastry, and the other made with plain flour, milk and ghee, more like a biscuit. I used egg wash to glaze them, but some use milk.

Preheat the oven to 200°C (180°C fan/400°F/gas 6).

On a lightly dusted work surface, roll out the puff pastry to a rectangle of about 30 x 10 cm (12 x 3 in), then cut lengthways into 5–6 long strips.

Roll up each strip into a swirl, then press with your palm to form a round about 3–4 cm (1–1¾ in) thick. Place them on a baking sheet. Brush with beaten egg and sprinkle with sugar. Bake in the oven for 12–15 minutes.

Serve with Kashmiri tea.

INGREDIENTS

PLAIN (ALL-PURPOSE) FLOUR, FOR DUSTING

300 G (10½ OZ) PUFF PASTRY (READY-MADE)

1 EGG, BEATEN

2 TEASPOONS DEMERARA SUGAR

LEFT AND BELOW
A small bakery, making traditional breads, where we stopped on our way to Pahalgam.

RIGHT
Kids playing outside the bakery.

KASHMIRI KULCHA

SWEET SPICY BREAD ROLL

MAKES 8

There are different kinds of kulchas. *I had a particularly delicious* kulcha *on my way to Pahalgam when we stopped in Anantnag, where they are famous for* kulchas. *This* kulcha *is small, hard, crumbly and round in shape. I use egg to glaze these, even though they usually use milk, as it gives a much nicer finish when baking at home.*

Crack the eggs into a small bowl, whisk and set aside.

In another bowl, combine the sugar and melted ghee, then add the egg mixture, whisk together and set aside.

In a mixing bowl, stir together the flour, crushed cardamom seeds, salt, baking powder and yeast. Add the sugar mixture and whisk in slowly, then knead to create dough. This takes around 5 minutes. Cover the bowl with a clean dish towel and leave to rest in a warm place for 1 hour.

Preheat the oven to 220°C (200°C fan/425°F/gas 7).

Divide the dough into 8 equal-sized balls. Flatten the balls and place on a baking sheet, then brush with the whisked egg yolk and sprinkle with sesame seeds. Bake in the oven for 12–15 minutes, until lovely and golden on the top.

INGREDIENTS

2 EGGS

100 G (3½ OZ/SCANT ½ CUP) CASTER (SUPERFINE) SUGAR

100 G (3½ OZ) GHEE

250 G (9 OZ/2 CUPS) PLAIN (ALL-PURPOSE) FLOUR

SEEDS OF 5 GREEN CARDAMOM PODS, CRUSHED TO A POWDER

½ TEASPOON SALT

½ TEASPOON BAKING POWDER

1 TEASPOON FAST-ACTION DRIED YEAST

3 TEASPOONS WHITE POPPY SEEDS OR SESAME SEEDS

LAVASA MASALA TCHOT

FLATBREADS STUFFED WITH SPLIT PEA
MASH AND CHUTNEY

MAKES 4

*Lavasa masalah, also known as masala tchot,
is a Kashmiri street-food wrap, filled with cooked yellow
split peas and spicy chutney. Some people apply butter
and jam to their lavasa.*

Start by making the flatbread dough. In a mixing bowl,
combine the flour with the salt, sugar and yeast, and mix.
Gradually add the lukewarm water and knead for 7–8
minutes to form a medium-soft dough. Cover the bowl
and leave to prove in a warm place for 1 hour.

Meanwhile, make the split pea mash. Drain, rinse, then
drain the peas again and place in a deep saucepan. Add
the rest of the mash ingredients and cook over a medium
heat, stirring, for 30 minutes until soft. Once the split
peas are cooked, drain well and set aside.

To make the chutney, add all the ingredients to a bowl.
Whisk to combine, then set aside.

Knock back the risen dough and knead for another
minute, then divide into 4 equal-sized balls.

Heat a heavy frying pan or cast-iron skillet until hot.

On a lightly floured work surface, roll out the dough
balls until they are 3–4 mm (⅛ in) thick and 7–8 cm
(3 in) in diameter. Apply water all over one of the discs
and place on the hot skillet. Cook until blisters form over
the surface of the bread, then upturn the pan and cook
the other side of the bread directly over the gas flame.

Repeat until all the breads are cooked.

To serve, spread the chutney and split pea mash over
each flatbread, then roll up and eat.

FOR THE FLATBREADS

150 G (5 OZ/1¼ CUPS) PLAIN (ALL-PURPOSE)
FLOUR, PLUS EXTRA FOR DUSTING

½ TEASPOON SALT

1 TEASPOON CASTER (SUPERFINE) SUGAR

1 TEASPOON FAST-ACTION DRIED YEAST

5–6 TABLESPOONS LUKEWARM WATER,
PLUS EXTRA AS NEEDED

FOR THE SPLIT PEA MASH

150 G (5 OZ/¾ CUP) DRIED WHITE SPLIT PEAS,
SOAKED OVERNIGHT

1 TEASPOON FRESHLY GROUND BLACK PEPPER

1 TEASPOON SALT

½ TEASPOON GROUND TURMERIC

½ TEASPOON GROUND CLOVES

700 ML (24 FL OZ/SCANT 3 CUPS) HOT WATER

FOR THE CHUTNEY

50 G (2 OZ) MOOLI (DAIKON/WHITE RADISHES),
PEELED AND GRATED

PINCH OF SALT

½ TEASPOON KASHMIRI CHILLI POWDER

100 G (3½ OZ/GENEROUS ⅓ CUP) GREEK
YOGHURT

A DAY OF
CELEBRATIONS

In the Sikh and Hindu calendars, April 13 2021 was an auspicious day. It marked the celebration of Vaisakhi: a harvest festival and the start of the solar new year for Hindus; and the celebration of the birth of Sikhism as a collective faith for Sikhs. To mark the occasion, I wanted to visit the Gurdwara Chati Patshahi – one of the most important Sikh pilgrimage sites in Kashmir. Situated in Ranawari, just outside the Kathi Darwaja (main entrance gate) of the Hari Parbat fort, it is named after the sixth Guru Shri, Guru Gobind Singh. Because of the celebrations, security was high, and they sensed that I was an outsider. My paperwork checked, they let me through to offer my prayers: a privilege on such a special occasion.

We carried on to the Sharika Devi temple, which can be found on the western slope of Srinagar's Hari Parbat, which overlooks Srinagar city and also offers an incredible view of Dal Lake. After being dropped off, we marched up the steps to the temple, saying our prayers in front of the structure before making our way to the top of the fort. Hari Parbat has the honour of being the only serving fort in Kashmir, built by Afghan governor Atta Mohammed Khan in 1808, building on a long outer wall that was originally put up by Mughal emperor Akbar in 1590. From here, you can see structures from all different religions, and the view from the top that day was incredible: so peaceful, so beautiful, and with more eagles than I've ever seen before swooping through the sky. I sat in one corner of the fort and looked down on the city through a window, picking out the Gurdwara and the shrine to Makhdoom Sahib, the well-respected Sufi mystic and spiritual teacher which was to be my next stop. As it was my last day in Kashmir, I was trying to fit everything in...

I was exhausted as I climbed the steps to Makhdoom Sahib's shrine, but I'm not one to give up. The shrine is open only to men, so I said my quiet prayers outside, and left feeling great. I'm of the firm belief that individuals and their religions should all be respected equally – it is the way my parents brought us up, and the way that I bring up my own girls, too.

AALCH CHETIN

SOUR CHERRY CHUTNEY

SERVES 4–6

INGREDIENTS

100 G (3½ OZ) SOUR CHERRIES
(SUCH AS MORELLO), WASHED

400 ML (13 FL OZ/GENEROUS 1½ CUPS) WATER

1 TEASPOON KASHMIRI CHILLI POWDER

PINCH OF ASAFOETIDA POWDER

½ TEASPOON SALT

4 TEASPOONS CASTER (SUPERFINE) SUGAR

*I have only ever had this chutney in Kashmir.
Kashmiri food is spicy and rich, and this chutney
is sweet and sour, which offers a balance when
eaten with other dishes.*

Place the cherries and water in a saucepan
and bring to the boil over a medium heat,
then cook for 15 minutes. Remove from the
heat and drain, then leave the cherries to cool.

Once the cherries are cool, crush with your
hands and remove the pits.

Place the cherries in a bowl, and add the
chilli powder, asafoetida, salt and sugar. Mix
really well and serve. Alternatively, use a food
processor, if you want your chutney smooth.

We make our chutneys fresh and eat
immediately with our food, but you can keep
this in the refrigerator for up to 2 weeks in an
airtight container.

ZIRISH CHETIN

BLACKCURRANT CHUTNEY

SERVES 4–6

INGREDIENTS

75 G (2½ OZ/SCANT ½ CUP) BLACKCURRANTS

50 G (2 OZ/GENEROUS ½ CUP) SULTANAS (GOLDEN RAISINS)

4 TEASPOONS TAMARIND PASTE DISSOLVED IN
3 TABLESPOONS WATER

1 TEASPOON KASHMIRI CHILLI POWDER

1 TEASPOON SALT

Zirish *chutney is full of exciting flavours – sweet,
tangy and spicy. It is hard work to make it in a
pestle and mortar, but it is well worth the effort.*

Soak the blackcurrants and sultanas separately
in water for 1 hour, then drain.

In a pestle and mortar, gently grind the
soaked blackcurrants and sultanas, then add
the rest of the ingredients and grind into a fine
paste. If you don't have a pestle and mortar, use
a blender – the texture will be a little different,
but it won't affect the taste.

We make our chutneys fresh and eat
immediately with our food, but you can keep
this in the refrigerator for up to 2 weeks in
an airtight container.

DOON CHETIN

WALNUT CHUTNEY

SERVES 4–6

INGREDIENTS

100 G (3½ OZ) SHELLED WALNUTS

3 RED KASHMIRI CHILLIES

1–2 SMALL GREEN CHILLIES

75 G (2½ OZ) ONION, CHOPPED

ZEST AND JUICE OF 1 LEMON

75 G (2½ OZ/SCANT ⅓ CUP) GREEK YOGHURT

1 TEASPOON SALT

Rich, creamy and nutty, this simple, flavourful walnut chutney can be used as a dip or a relish. It is traditionally prepared in a pestle and mortar, but you can make it in a food processor.

Soak the walnuts and red chillies separately in water for about 1 hour, then drain.

In a pestle and mortar, combine the soaked walnuts and red chillies with the green chillies, onion, and lemon zest and juice. Pound until you get an even consistency. If you don't have a pestle and mortar, use a blender.

Transfer the mixture to a bowl, then fold in the yoghurt and salt and mix well.

We make our chutneys fresh and eat immediately with our food, but you can keep this in the refrigerator for up to 1 week in an airtight container.

GAND CHETIN

SHALLOT RELISH

SERVES 4

INGREDIENTS

250 G (9 OZ) SMALL ROUND SHALLOTS, PEELED AND THINLY SLICED

1–2 TEASPOONS SALT

100 ML (3½ FL OZ/SCANT ½ CUP) MALT VINEGAR

5–6 BIRD'S EYE OR SMALL GREEN CHILLIES

HANDFUL OF FRESH CORIANDER (CILANTRO), CHOPPED

1 TEASPOON KASHMIRI CHILLI POWDER

½ TEASPOON DRIED MINT

I had this shallot relish in a hotel in Srinagar and was kindly given the recipe by the hotel chef.

Place the shallots in a bowl. Sprinkle with 1 teaspoon of the salt and set aside for 5 minutes.

After 5 minutes, wash the shallots under running water and drain.

Add the remaining igredients to the bowl and stir to combine, then serve.

You can keep this relish in an airtight container in the refrigerator for few days.

RADISH RAITA   PAGE 196

PUMPKIN RELISH   PAGE 196

MUJ DOUD DAR

RADISH RAITA

SERVES 4–5

INGREDIENTS

200 G (7 OZ) RADISHES (IDEALLY MOOLI/DAIKON)

200 G (7 OZ/GENEROUS ¾ CUP) GREEK YOGHURT

1 TEASPOON SALT

1 GREEN CHILLI, FINELY CHOPPED

¼ TEASPOON BLACK CUMIN SEEDS

½ TEASPOON FRESHLY GROUND BLACK PEPPER

This is made with white mooli (daikon), but if you cannot find them, use regular radishes. With the white mooli, we either peel or scrape the skin; with small pink or purple radishes we don't need to.

Wash, peel and grate the mooli, then squeeze out as much water as possible and place in a bowl. Add the yoghurt, salt, chilli, black cumin seeds and pepper, and whisk it all together. Serve as a side dish with your meal.

DODH AAL

PUMPKIN RELISH

SERVES 4–5

INGREDIENTS

200 G (7 OZ) PUMPKIN (SQUASH), PEELED AND DICED INTO CHUNKS

6 GARLIC CLOVES

50 G (2 OZ/SCANT ¼ CUP) YOGHURT

1½ TABLESPOONS SULTANAS (GOLDEN RAISINS)

1 TABLESPOON HONEY

½ TEASPOON SALT

PINCH OF SAFFRON STRANDS

PINCH OF BLACK CUMIN SEEDS

This is simple yet delightful. Steamed and mashed pumpkin is combined with creamy yoghurt and gentle spicing, to create a relish that is a real treat to enjoy as a side dish, with your food.

Place the pumpkin and garlic cloves in a saucepan. Cover with water and boil under tender, then drain and let cool.
    Mash the pumpkin, then transfer the mash to a muslin (cheesecloth) and squeeze out any excess water.
    Place the mash in a bowl with rest of the ingredients and mix together.

MONJ AACHAR

KOHLRABI PICKLE

SERVES AT LEAST 8–10

INGREDIENTS

500 G (1 LB 2 OZ) KOHLRABI, WASHED, PEELED AND
CUT INTO 4 CM (1¾ IN) PIECES

200 ML (7 FL OZ/SCANT 1 CUP) MUSTARD OIL OR
RAPESEED (CANOLA) OIL

1 TEASPOON ASAFOETIDA POWDER

100 G (3½ OZ/⅔ CUP) BLACK MUSTARD SEEDS, CRUSHED

1 TABLESPOON KASHMIRI CHILLI POWDER

2 TEASPOONS GROUND GINGER

2 TEASPOONS GROUND FENNEL

2 TEASPOONS SALT

*Pickles are huge part of Indian culture – we enjoy
them with most meals. In Kashmir, vegetables
are dried to enjoy out of season, and pickles are
made for the same reason. Monj Aachar is not
complicated to make, but it is delicious to eat.*

Place the kohlrabi pieces on a plate lined with
paper towels. Cover with a dish towel and leave
for at least 2 days so all the moisture comes out.
In India, people sometimes leave it out in the
sun to dry.

Heat the oil in a deep saucepan over a
medium heat. Add the asafoetida, spices and
salt and cook for 1 minute, then add the dried
kohlrabi and mix together thoroughly.

Transfer to a sterilised jar with an airtight
lid. Store in the sun or in a warm place for
1 week before eating.

Serve with your meals.

CHHIEAR AACHAR

APRICOT PICKLE

SERVES AT LEAST 8–10

INGREDIENTS

500 G (1 LB 2 OZ) FIRM APRICOTS, WASHED AND DRIED

100 ML (3½ FL OZ/SCANT ½ CUP) MUSTARD OIL OR
RAPESEED (CANOLA) OIL

½ TEASPOON ASAFOETIDA POWDER

1 TEASPOON GROUND TURMERIC

1 TEASPOON GROUND GINGER

1–2 TEASPOONS KASHMIRI CHILLI POWDER

1–2 TEASPOONS SALT

2 TEASPOONS CASTER (SUPERFINE) SUGAR

*Amit told me that this apricot pickle is very
typical of Kashmir. Make sure your apricots
are firm for this recipe.*

Prick the apricots with a toothpick or fork
and set aside.

Heat the oil in a saucepan over a medium
heat. Add the asafoetida, spices, salt and sugar,
and cook for 1 minute, then add the apricots
and turn to coat in the spices.

Transfer to a sterilised jar with an airtight
lid. Store in the sun or in a warm place for
1 week before eating. Serve with your meals.

LADAKH

LEH

LEARNING MORE
ABOUT LADAKH

In the early days of my relationship with my husband Gundeep, he would tell me tales of his travels throughout India. The stories I always remembered best were those about Leh, and how he travelled there via scooter from Punjab with his friends. The way he described Leh's remoteness and its landscape filled me with a great desire to visit. Until fairly recently, though, I had never had the chance. So, when the opportunity came to visit Ladakh, the territory in which Leh is the largest town, on a press trip, I immediately said yes, and decided to make the journey with my family.

It was then that I met Dadul, a local who was to be my guide, for the first time. Welcoming us to Ladakh, he described it as 'the land of high passes'. It is part of the wider Jammu and Kashmir region, bordered on the east by Tibet, and to the south by the Lahaul and Spiti district of Himachal Pradesh. With the Kunkun mountains in the north and the Himalayas in the south, and located on the country's ancient trade routes, it's not only an important part of India, but one whose scenery is so different compared with everywhere else in India. Its landscapes are so barren, yet so beautiful.

Because of its strategic location, the Indian army still has a strong presence in Ladakh – and Gundeep had told me that the area could not be visited by tourists until around the 1970s. Its proximity to Tibet means that the majority of Ladakhis are Tibetan Buddhists, but the region's inhabitants fall into three main groups: those of Tibetan descent, Indo-Aryans and Shia Muslims.

The vividly descriptive stories Gundeep had shared with me over the years all turned out to be accurate. I fell in love with Ladakh's scenic beauty. The rugged landscapes of the car journey, the mountains of all different shapes and sizes, picture-perfect *gompas* (Tibetan temples), flags fluttering in the wind, white-painted *stupas* (Buddhist monuments): there were so many different sights to be awed by. I was so inspired by the spectacular beauty of this remote location that I plan to make a return trip to go camping to explore the wilder parts of the region – something I've never done before.

One thing that struck me was how different the definition of 'sustainability' is between the UK and Ladakh. In the UK, it's something to strive for – something which, for the most part, people have to make significant life changes in order to achieve. In Ladakh, however, people simply live sustainably with what they have. Many still live in homesteads traditionally crafted from mud bricks, and producing crops or products with which to sustain your household – particularly grains, such as barley, and dairy products – is the norm.

The extreme climate of Ladakh, an area that experiences frequent snowfall, means that many vegetables and other crops simply can't grow. Peas, beans, turnips, potatoes, beetroot and pumpkins are some of the most common vegetables of the region, and buckwheat, millet, wheat and barley are among the most common crops. The latter is a staple part of the Ladakhi diet, roasted and ground into a flour called *tsampa*, which is used to make soups and dumpling wrappers, and is often also stirred into salty butter tea (page 236).

Ladakh has been a region associated mostly with the Maggi bouillion empire and *momo* dumplings (page 204), but I was soon to learn that there is far more to the area's cuisine than that...

I had the pleasure of tasting *Chhurpi* – a type of yak cheese –on my travels to Leh. It is made from the domesticated yak, called Dzomo, which is a hybrid between a yak and a cow. The cheese tastes very similar to ricotta and there are two varieties found. One is hard and other soft. It is essential in the local diet, and is used as a filling in *momos* and in *thukpa* (soups, page 208).

MOMOS

DUMPLINGS

MAKES 30

Momos are famous in Ladakhi cuisine. These filled dumplings can have a variety of different stuffings – meat, vegetables or paneer – and can be either fried or steamed (in a traditional steamer called a mokto*). They come in a few different shapes and are eaten with chilli sauce or served as an accompaniment to soup. They can be eaten at any time of day and are found across all the Himalayan regions of India. This recipe was taught to me by Charol's mother-in-law, Palzes (or Palay, as her family call her), on my first trip to Ladakh.*

To make the dough, sift the flour into a bowl and add a pinch of salt. Gradually add the water, mixing and kneading until you have a flexible dough. Drizzle the oil over the dough, turning it to coat, cover with a dish towel and leave to rest for 20–30 minutes at room temperature.

Meanwhile, make the filling. Place all the ingredients in a bowl and mix to combine.

Divide the dough into about 30 equal-sized balls, each weighing around 10–12 g (½ oz). Dust the work surface with flour, then roll one of the balls into thin circles, about 8 cm (3 in) in diameter, one at a time. Place 1 heaped teaspoon of the filling mixture in the middle of each circle of dough, then use your thumb and forefinger to pinch the sides together to seal each parcel.

Repeat until all the dough and filling are used up.

Fill a steamer pan with water, cover the base of the steamer with baking paper and pierce a few holes in it. Place over a high heat and bring to the boil.

Working in batches, place the *momos* on the baking paper, cover the pan with the lid and steam for 10–12 minutes until the *momos* look transparent.

FOR THE DOUGH

300 G (10½ OZ/2½ CUPS) ATTA CHAPATI FLOUR (OR PLAIN/ALL-PURPOSE), PLUS EXTRA FOR DUSTING

PINCH OF SALT

190–200 ML (6½–7 FL OZ/⅔–SCANT 1 CUP) WATER, AT ROOM TEMPERATURE

2 TEASPOONS SUNFLOWER OIL

FOR THE FILLING

30 G (1 OZ) WHITE CABBAGE, FINELY GRATED

30 G (1 OZ) CARROT, PEELED AND FINELY GRATED

30 G (1 OZ) POTATOES, PEELED AND FINELY GRATED

20 G (¾ OZ) ONION, FINELY CHOPPED

20 G (¾ OZ) SPINACH, FINELY CHOPPED

1 GREEN CHILLI, CHOPPED

1 TEASPOON GROUND CORIANDER

1 TEASPOON SALT

THUKPA

NOODLE SOUP

SERVES 3

All Ladakhis love thukpa, *although it is also popular in other regions of the Himalayas. It is a clear soup with vegetables, noodles made of wheat or barley flour, and chicken, mutton or yak meat. You can just leave out the meat if you prefer it vegetarian. It is usually served with spicy chutney to bring out the flavours.*

To make the noodle dough, sift the flour into a bowl, then gradually add the water and knead into a soft dough. Leave to rest for 5 minutes.

If you're including chicken, heat the oil in a sauté pan over a medium heat, then add the chicken strips and cook for 10 minutes until browned on all sides. Set aside.

Dust the work surface with flour and roll the noodle dough into a thin sheet, around 2 mm in thickness, (or put it through a pasta machine), then cut into long, thin noodles. Set aside while you start the broth.

In a separate, large saucepan over a high heat, combine the water, carrots, mooli, peas and salt. Bring to the boil, then cook for 4–5 minutes. Stir the cooked chicken (if using) into the pan, along with the spring onions and spinach. Add the noodles to the pan and cook for 8–10 minutes over a medium heat.

To make the temper, heat the oil in a small pan over a medium heat. When hot, add the garlic, chives, caraway seeds and black pepper, and mix together.

Pour the hot temper into the broth and mix through. Serve hot, spooned into bowls, and topped with the yak cheese or Parmesan crumbled over.

FOR THE NOODLE DOUGH

100 G (3½ OZ/GENEROUS ¾ CUP) ATTA CHAPATI FLOUR (OR PLAIN/ALL-PURPOSE)

80-100 ML (2¾-3½ FL OZ/5½ - 6½ TABLESPOONS) WATER

FOR THE BROTH

2 TEASPOONS MUSTARD OIL OR SUNFLOWER OIL (OPTIONAL)

1 CHICKEN BREAST, CUT INTO THIN STRIPS (OPTIONAL)

500 ML (17 FL OZ/2 CUPS) WATER

50 G (2 OZ) CARROTS, PEELED AND CUT INTO THIN BATONS

50 G (2 OZ) MOOLI (DAIKON/RADISH), PEELED AND CUT INTO THIN BATONS

50 G (2 OZ/⅓ CUP) PEAS

1 TEASPOON SALT

4 SPRING ONIONS (SCALLIONS), WHITES AND GREENS CHOPPED

75 G (2½ OZ) SPINACH, ROUGHLY CHOPPED

1 TEASPOON DRIED YAK CHEESE (FOUND ONLINE) OR CRUMBLED PARMESAN

FOR THE TEMPER

2 TEASPOONS MUSTARD OIL OR VEGETABLE OIL

3 GARLIC CLOVES, CHOPPED

1 TEASPOON CHIVES, CHOPPED

1 TEASPOON CARAWAY SEEDS

1 TEASPOON FRESHLY GOUND BLACK PEPPER

BREATHTAKING –
A FARMSTAY IN LADAKH

How do you normally travel? Some love the comfort and ease of having a hotel or B&B room to go back to at the end of each day. Others relish the thrill of camping under the stars. For others still it's the freedom of a self-catering property that appeals: being able to cook your own meals and essentially have a home away from home is nice!

But there are other options too. In Europe, agricultural tourism: staying on working farms to gain an experience of what traditional local farming life is all about. I hadn't realised that these 'farmstays' were possible in India, though, and I was excited to learn all about how Ladakhi innovator and mechanical engineer, Sonam Wangchuk, had introduced the concept.

It was an honour to meet him and hear from that passionate, community-spirited and truly entrepreneurial man the story of Indian farmstays. When he first started thinking about the idea, it was to solve a problem. Younger people were leaving their villages in droves, looking for careers and financial success in the big cities instead. It meant that the older members of their families had nobody to help with running the farms – nor anyone look after these family members themselves.

Sonam's question was: 'How can we encourage younger generations to stay in their village and keep things running smoothly?' He realised that they'd need to be persuaded by a career choice that was exciting as well as lucrative – and something that could benefit their community as a whole. And so, the farmstay concept was born.

At first, seven farmers in Phyang village signed up to the scheme, agreeing to rent out rooms on their farms as tourist accommodation for visitors who wanted to really live local village life. Over the years, the number has grown and grown – and now includes Charol and her family, who I stayed with when I was there.

As soon as she learned that I was a chef, that was it: food was the topic of conversation for much of my stay! It was great to hear her speak so passionately, not just about how she prepares food for her family and guests, but also how the farm and the village is run from an agricultural perspective. Most of what her family grows on their farm is sent off to the city to be sold, while the rest of the food is for her family and their guests.

She kindly invited me into her kitchen to learn more about their food culture, and it was wonderful to see, learn and experience how the simplest of ingredients, picked freshly from their own land, can be transformed into such a huge variety of delicious dishes. I sat with Charol, her husband and her mother-in-law to learn how to make *momos* (dumplings) – I'll never make them with the speed they do! I watched as she magicked up a steaming pan of fragrant carrot and spinach soup, and I took notes as she demonstrated how to make their favourite spicy fermented pickles.

I urge anyone with a love of local food to book a farmstay when visiting this part of India. You're treated like a member of the family, you learn about what village life really involves, and you get a detailed understanding of what genuine local food is all about. I left with a great experience of daily life in a region I had known very little about – and also with a renewed sense of wanting to make the same effort to revitalise my own local community.

SKYU

Skyu is the traditional speciality and staple food of Ladakhi cuisine. I was lucky enough to try it at the farmstay visit, on my first trip to Leh. It is a pasta made of wheat flour, which is served with a vegetable broth. The pasta dough is shaped into small thumb-imprinted discs and is then slow-cooked with the root vegetables. Some cooks also use mutton and mutton bones to enrich the broth. This dish has been enjoyed in the villages for centuries and is perfect for the harsh winters. Dadul, our guide for both trips who used to work for Sonam, explained to me that in the villages they also add milk, although I have made it without here.

To make the pasta dough, sift the flour into a bowl, slowly add the water and knead into a soft dough. Leave to rest for 5 minutes.

Dust the work surface with flour and roll out the pasta dough into a thin sheet, 2 mm thick and around 15 cm (6 in) in diameter (or put it through a pasta machine). Cut the sheet into long, thick strips, then cut each strip into small equal-sized pieces. Roll each piece into a ball, then pinch each one almost flat with your thumb and forefinger. Repeat with all the dough and set aside while you start the broth.

To make the broth, heat the oil in a large saucepan over a medium heat. When hot, add the onions and ginger, and cook for 5 minutes. Stir through the green chillies and salt, then add all the vegetables and cook for 2 minutes.

Add the water and bring to the boil, then reduce the heat to low, cover and cook until the vegetables are soft.

Finally, add the pasta to the broth and cook for a final 5 minutes. Enjoy hot, garnished with coriander leaves, if you like.

FOR THE PASTA DOUGH

250 G (9 OZ/2 CUPS) ATTA CHAPATI FLOUR (OR PLAIN/ALL-PURPOSE), PLUS EXTRA FOR DUSTING

ABOUT 125 ML (4 FL OZ/½ CUP) WATER

FOR THE BROTH

2–3 TEASPOONS SUNFLOWER OIL

75 G (2½ OZ) ONIONS, CHOPPED

8 G (¼ OZ) FRESH GINGER ROOT, GRATED

1–2 GREEN CHILLIES, CHOPPED

1 TEASPOON SALT

75 G (2½ OZ) TOMATOES, CHOPPED

100 G (3½ OZ) POTATOES, PEELED AND DICED INTO 1 CM (½ IN) CHUNKS

100 G (3½ OZ) CARROTS, PEELED AND DICED INTO 1 CM (½ IN) CHUNKS

100 G (3½ OZ) TURNIPS, PEELED AND DICED INTO 1 CM (½ IN) CHUNKS

50 G (2 OZ/⅓ CUP) PEAS

500 ML (17 FL OZ/2 CUPS) WATER

SMALL HANDFUL OF FRESH CORIANDER (CILANTRO) LEAVES, TO GARNISH (OPTIONAL), ROUGHLY CHOPPED

TOP
Shanti Stupa Monastery in Leh.

LEFT
Two monks in Phyang Monastery.

RIGHT
Local woman praying at the Alchi Monastery.

ZATHUK

STINGING NETTLE SOUP

SERVES 3–4

This is the vegetarian version of this soup according to Kunzes Angmo, who runs Artisanal Alchemy. In the past, the non-vegetarian version was more common: a lump of animal fat (from a goat, sheep, yak or dzo) would be melted, and then the soup would be cooked in it. If you want it a little thicker, you can add more roasted barley flour, although I find that overpowers the flavour. Dried nettles are easily sourced online.

Bring the measured water to the boil in a large saucepan, add the nettles and boil for 35 minutes.

Add the butter or ghee or lard and the salt and pepper, then add the roasted barley flour, stirring constantly with a whisk to avoid any lumps forming. Sprinkle in the Chinese celery and boil for a further 15–20 minutes until the soup has thickened slightly.

Strain the soup before serving and enjoy with flatbreads.

INGREDIENTS

LITRE (34 FL OZ/4 CUPS) WATER

75 G (2½ OZ) DRIED WILD STINGING NETTLES, WASHED (IF USING FRESH, USE GLOVES AND SHRED BEFORE USE)

1 TABLESPOON BUTTER, GHEE OR LARD

1 TEASPOON SALT

½ TEASPOON FRESHLY GROUND BLACK PEPPER

4 TEASPOONS ROASTED BARLEY FLOUR (SGNAMPHEY IN LADAKHI AND TSAMPA IN TIBETAN, AVAILABLE FROM ASIAN GROCERS OR ONLINE)

½ TEASPOON DRIED CHINESE CELERY (AVAILABLE FROM ASIAN GROCERS OR ONLINE)

FLATBREADS, TO SERVE

LEFT
Breathtaking views on the way to Kargil.

ABOVE
Chutagi (page 220).

CHUTAGI

PASTA WITH VEGETABLES

SERVES 3–4

Chutagi is a famous Ladakhi dish, like pasta with a rich vegetable sauce. Chu means water in Ladakh and tagi means bread. The pasta dough is made in the shape of a bow-tie, and is cooked in a thick soup of potatoes, carrots and local leafy green vegetables. There is a version made with mutton as well.

To make the pasta dough, sift the flour into a bowl, slowly add the water and knead into a soft dough. Leave to rest for at least 10 minutes.

Dust the work surface with flour and roll the pasta dough into a 2 mm thin sheet (or put it through a pasta machine). Roll to around 20 cm (8 in) long. Use a 5 cm (2 in) cookie cutter to cut small rounds out of the pasta sheet. Wrap each pasta circle around your index finger and pinch the tube closed. Gently pull your finger out, then pinch the two open ends of the tube together. It should resemble two cones joined at the bottom. Repeat until all the dough is used up and set aside.

To make the broth, place the lamb and 500 ml (17 fl oz/2 cups) of the water in a saucepan. Bring to the boil and until the meat is tender, about 30–40 minutes.

Meanwhile, heat the oil in a separate deep saucepan over a medium heat. When hot, add the garlic and onion, and cook for 4–5 minutes. Add the rest of the vegetables and cook for about 2 minutes, then add the salt, pepper and chilli powder, along with the remaining 200 ml (7 fl oz/scant 1 cup) of water. Cook for 15 minutes until the vegetables are tender.

Finally, add the cooked lamb and pasta to the broth and cook for a final 10 minutes until the pasta is chewy, firm and holding its shape. Serve hot.

FOR THE PASTA DOUGH

100 G (3½ OZ/GENEROUS ¾ CUPS) ATTA CHAPATI FLOUR (OR PLAIN/ALL-PURPOSE), PLUS EXTRA FOR DUSTING

ABOUT 75 ML (2½ FL OZ/5 TABLESPOONS) WATER, AT ROOM TEMPERATURE

FOR THE BROTH

250 G (9 OZ) BONELESS LAMB

700 ML (24 FL OZ/SCANT 3 CUPS) WATER

4 TEASPOONS MUSTARD OIL OR SUNFLOWER OIL

4 GARLIC CLOVES, CHOPPED

75 G (2½ OZ) WHITE ONION, CHOPPED

75 G (2½ OZ) POTATOES, PEELED AND DICED

75 G (2½ OZ) CARROTS, PEELED AND DICED

75 G (2½ OZ) LEAFY GREENS, ROUGHLY CHOPPED

75 G (2½ OZ) KOHLRABI, PEELED AND DICED

100 G (3½ OZ) TOMATOES, CHOPPED

1 TEASPOON SALT

½ TEASPOON FRESHLY GROUND BLACK PEPPER

½ TEASPOON CHILLI POWDER

TINGMO

STEAMED BREAD

MAKES 8

Tingmo require patience, but at the same time are very satisfying to make. These Tibetan steamed buns are a delicate, soft and fluffy bun, made with wheat flour, which is served with vegetables, meat and dal. There are many ways of making tingmo, but this is the easiest technique I've found. You can watch many videos online, to see the folding and stretching technique. Once it is steamed, all the layers of the bun seem to fluff up and open.

In a large mixing bowl, mix together the flour, salt, sugar and yeast, then slowly add the water (you may not need it all). Mix to a dough, then knead, folding, rotating and stretching until the dough comes together and is soft. Drizzle 2 teaspoons of oil over the ball of dough, turning it to coat, then cover with a wet dish towel and leave to rest for 1 hour.

Use the remaining 1 teaspoon of oil, oil a kitchen surface suitable for rolling out the dough. Then, use a rolling pin to roll the dough uniformly in all directions, to create a rectangular shape about 45 x 40 cm (18 x 16 in). Fold the dough into thirds, lengthways, then divide the folded length of dough into 4 equal parts. Divide each quarter further into 6 equal strips. Stack the strips in groups of three, so that you now have 4 sets of strips. To form the *tingmo*, pick one stack, then stretch it, twist it and swirl it into a round shape. Cover and leave to prove for 30 minutes.

Line a steamer basket with a sheet of baking paper with some holes cut into it. Place the *tingmo* in the prepared steamer and steam for 20 minutes. Don't overcook them, as they will become rubbery in texture.

INGREDIENTS

250 G (9 OZ/2 CUPS) PLAIN (ALL-PURPOSE) FLOUR

½ TEASPOON SALT

1 TEASPOON CASTER (SUPERFINE) SUGAR

3 G (1 TEASPOON) FAST-ACTION DRIED YEAST

UP TO 150 ML (5 FL OZ/SCANT ⅔ CUP) LUKEWARM WATER

3 TEASPOONS SUNFLOWER OIL

KHAMBIR

FERMENTED WHEAT BREAD

MAKES 6

This fermented wheat-based bread is baked over a hot stone, then finished directly on the fire. It's delicious when it is freshly baked and warm. Ladakhi people eat khambir *with eggs or vegetables for breakfast. It is also eaten with Butter Tea (page 236). The best thing about this bread is that you can keep it at room temperature for a week. Some people stuff the breads with herby, buttery mashed potatoes, chhurpi* (yak cheese), *dried apricots or jam.*

In a large mixing bowl, combine the flour and salt, then sprinkle the yeast all over and mix in. Gradually add the hot water and start to bring the dough together, folding and kneading until the dough is soft. Place the dough in an airtight container and leave in a warm place overnight or for 10–12 hours.

The next day, divide the dough into 6 equal-sized balls. On a lightly floured surface, roll each ball out into a disc, 3 mm (⅛ in) thick and about 5 cm (2 in) in diameter.

Heat a dry *tawa* or frying pan (skillet) over a medium heat until hot.

Place the first flatbread on the hot pan and cook on both sides until blisters form, then use tongs to place it directly over a gas flame and let it puff up. Repeat with the remaining flatbreads.

Serve immediately.

INGREDIENTS

400 G (14 OZ/3¼ CUPS) ATTA CHAPATI FLOUR, PLUS EXTRA FOR DUSTING (YOU CAN ALSO USE PLAIN FLOUR, IF YOU LIKE)

1 TEASPOON SALT

4 G (1¼ TEASPOONS) FAST-ACTION DRIED YEAST

175 ML (6 FL OZ/¾ CUP) HOT WATER

PABA WITH TANGTUR

ROASTED FLOUR BREAD WITH SPICED
BUTTERMILK

SERVES 4

Paba *is an uncooked bread-like mixture of roasted wheat
flour, barley flour, pea flour and turtle bean flour. I was told
that if you can't get hold of this last flour, then you can mix
in buckwheat flour instead. The toasted flours are cooked in
water and not baked in the oven. It is very sticky consistency
and is delicious with* Tangtur, *a sort of buttermilk dip,
flavoured with seasonal greens.*

*This recipe was given to me by Kunzes Angmo and
Nilza Wangmo. Kunzes said that in Ladakh they use
any greens depending on the season. The most common is*
saganik, *also called* sagan, *which is* bhatua *leaves – a weed
that is dried for winter for use specifically in this dish. It is
common in Himachal and Uttarakhand. Those who are not
able to get* saganik *use other greens instead, such as rocket
(arugula), mustard leaves or spinach.*

For the *paba*, toast the flours in a dry pan over a very low
heat until they smell warm and toasted. Remove from the
heat and set aside in a bowl.

In a wok, bring the water and salt to the boil over a
high heat, then reduce the heat to medium and add the
toasted flour. Mix and leave the ladle or spatula in the
pan so the mixture doesn't overflow. When all the water
has been absorbed by the flour mixture, stir and scrape
the mixture and shape into 2 dough pieces – traditionally
they are made into a kind of trangle shape. Transfer to
a plate.

For the *tangtur*, blanch the greens in boiling water,
then drain. Place the buttermilk in a bowl and stir in
the blanched greens.

Heat the mustard oil in a frying pan (skillet) over
a medium heat. Add the dried chives and caraway seeds,
then, as soon they start to sizzle, remove from the heat.
Pour over the buttermilk mixture, season with the salt,
mix together and enjoy with the *paba*.

FOR THE PABA

50 G (2 OZ/GENEROUS ⅓ CUP) BARLEY FLOUR

50 G (2 OZ/GENEROUS ⅓ CUP) ATTA
CHAPATI FLOUR

50 G (2 OZ/GENEROUS ⅓ CUP)
BROWN OR GREEN PEA FLOUR

50 G (2 OZ/GENEROUS ⅓ CUP) TURTLE BEAN
FLOUR (OR BUCKWHEAT FLOUR)

350 ML (12 FL OZ/SCANT 1½ CUPS) WATER

1 TEASPOON SALT

FOR THE TANGTUR

HANDFUL OF SEASONAL GREENS, CHOPPED

250 ML (8½ FL OZ/1 CUP) BUTTERMILK

2 TEASPOONS MUSTARD OIL

2 TEASPOONS DRIED CHIVES

½ TEASPOON CARAWAY SEEDS

½ TEASPOON SALT

TAIN TAIN WITH WALNUT CHUTNEY

BUCKWHEAT PANCAKES
WITH WALNUT CHUTNEY

SERVES 3

This recipe was cooked for me by Nilza Wangmo, from Alchi Kitchen in Ladakh. She makes these amazing buckwheat pancakes, along with many other delicious dishes. You must make the pancakes immediately after whisking the batter, because if left for too long, the buckwheat becomes very sticky and stodgy. Nilza also made us this delicious, creamy walnut chutney to go with the pancakes. It is very different to the walnut chutney of Kashmir (see Doon Chetin on page 192).

To make the pancake batter, whisk the egg in a bowl and add a pinch of salt, then gradually add the flour and caraway seeds and mix well. Add the water and whisk until you have a smooth batter.

Heat a non-stick frying pan (skillet) over a medium heat. Once the pan is hot, brush evenly with oil or butter, then carefully add a ladleful of the batter and immediately spread with the back of the ladle to form a pancake. Cook for 2–3 minutes, then brush a little oil or butter on top, flip and cook the other side. Repeat the process with the remaining batter.

To make the chutney, place all the ingredients in a small food processor and blitz to a paste.

Serve the hot pancakes with the chutney.

FOR THE PANCAKES

1 EGG

PINCH OF SALT

150 G (5 OZ/SCANT 1¼ CUPS) BUCKWHEAT FLOUR

1 TEASPOON CARAWAY SEEDS

220 ML (8 FL OZ/SCANT 1 CUP) WATER

BUTTER, MUSTARD OIL OR RAPESEED (CANOLA)OIL, FOR COOKING

FOR THE WALNUT CHUTNEY

75 G (2½ OZ) SHELLED WALNUTS

3 SPRING ONIONS (SCALLIONS), WHITES AND GREENS ROUGHLY CHOPPED

JUICE OF ½ LEMON

1 TABLESPOON SUNFLOWER OIL OR RAPESEED (CANOLA) OIL

½ TEASPOON CHILLI FLAKES

½ TEASPOON SALT

LEFT
The flying flags of the Namgyal Tsemo
Gompa in Leh.

ABOVE
The vibrant red painted window with a bright
yellow curtain of the Thiksey Monastery.

YARKHANDI PULAO

RICE WITH CARROTS, FRUIT AND MEAT

SERVES 8

I had this pulao at Kunzes and at Nilza places in Leh and loved the sweetness of the dried fruits with the fatty lamb. This dish travelled all the way from Yarkhand to Ladakh along the southern tributaries of the ancient Silk Road, and was a novelty decades ago before rice was commonly available. The rice is cooked with big chunks of meat with plenty of fat, julienned local baby carrots (preserved in a root cellar), slivers of fried onion and aromatic whole spices. It's dressed with roasted nuts and black raisins. It is most similar to Afghani and Mongolian pilafs. The carrots not only give sweetness to the pulao, but also lend a beautiful pale orange colour to the rice.

Pour the water into a large pan over a high heat, add the lamb along with 1 teaspoon of the salt, and boil for 20–25 minutes until the meat is half cooked. Skim off and discard any scum that rises to the surface. Remove from the heat, strain the cooking water into a jug and set the meat aside.

Meanwhile, about 10 minutes into the lamb's cooking time, place the rice in a separate saucepan. Add the remaining 1 teaspoon of salt and cover with water. Bring to the boil and cook for 3 minutes. Drain, then spread the rice on a dish towel or paper towels to dry out.

Heat the ghee in a separate large saucepan with a lid over a medium heat. Add all the whole spices and the bay leaves and fry for 1 minute, then add the part-cooked lamb and cook for 3–4 minutes until the meat is browned all over. Add the grated carrots, dried apricots and raisins and cook for another 2 minutes.

Reduce the heat to low, then layer the part-cooked rice on top of the meat and pour over 100 ml (3½ fl oz/scant ½ cup) of the reserved cooking stock. Cover the pan with a tight lid and cook for 15–20 minutes.

Serve hot.

INGREDIENTS

1.5 LITRES (50 FL OZ/6 CUPS) WATER

750 G (1 LB 10 OZ) FATTY LAMB ON THE BONE, CUT INTO BITE-SIZED PIECES

2 TEASPOONS SALT

500 G (1 LB 2 OZ/2½ CUPS) BASMATI RICE

4 TEASPOONS GHEE

8 CM (3 IN) CINNAMON STICK

4 GREEN CARDAMOM PODS

4 BLACK CARDAMOM PODS

8 BLACK PEPPERCORNS

2 BAY LEAVES

300 G (10½ OZ) CARROTS, PEELED AND GRATED

100 G (3½ OZ/GENEROUS ½ CUP) DRIED APRICOTS

100 G (3½ OZ/ GENEROUS ¾ CUP) RAISINS

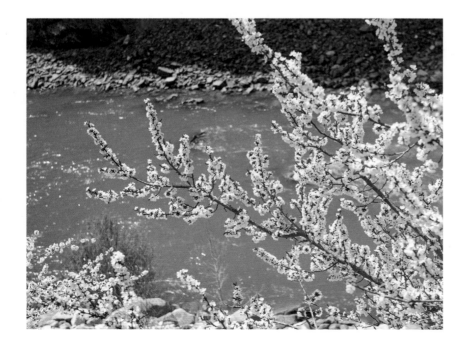

LADAKHI ACHAR

LADAKHI PICKLE

MAKES 1 X 1 LITRE (34 FL OZ) JAR

INGREDIENTS

300 ML (10 FL OZ/1¼ CUPS) MUSTARD OIL

150 G (5 OZ) CARROTS, PEELED AND ROUGHLY CHOPPED

150 G (5 OZ) KOHLRABI, PEELED AND ROUGHLY CHOPPED

150 G (5 OZ) RADISHES, PEELED AND ROUGHLY CHOPPED

100 G (3½ OZ) TURNIPS, PEELED AND ROUGHLY CHOPPED

2 TEASPOONS FENNEL SEEDS, TOASTED AND CRUSHED

2 TEASPOONS CORIANDER SEEDS, TOASTED AND CRUSHED

1 TEASPOON BLACK CUMIN SEEDS

15 BLACK PEPPERCORNS

2 TEASPOONS MUSTARD SEEDS

2 TEASPOONS KASHMIRI CHILLI POWDER

2 TEASPOONS SALT

For this pickle, carrots, cabbage, kohlrabi, radishes and turnips are used. Pickles are a very important part of any Indian cuisine and every part of India has their own way of making the pickles. Ladakh is known for its harsh winters so most of the vegetables grown or bought are pickled to enjoy later.

First, heat the mustard oil in a saucepan. When the oil is smoking hot, remove from the heat and set aside to cool.

Place all the chopped vegetables in a pan, cover with boiling water and blanch for 15 minutes. Drain and spread over a dish towel to dry them out as thoroughly as possible.

Transfer all the vegetables to a bowl and add all the spices and salt. Pour 100 ml (3½ fl oz/ scant ½ cup) of the mustard oil on top and give it good mix, so everything is well coated.

Transfer to a clean glass jar with an airtight lid. Pour over the remaining mustard oil and seal. Store in the refrigerator and enjoy within 7 days.

KHUBANI

DRIED APRICOTS

SERVES 4

INGREDIENTS

20 DRIED APRICOTS

100 ML (3½ FL OZ/SCANT ½ CUP) WATER

1 TEASPOON SUGAR

The dried apricots from this region have the most intense sweet flavour in the world. The variety is called Raktsey Karpo *and it is unique to Ladakh. Locally, they dry the fresh apricots and serve as dessert during celebrations or traditional festivals. When steeped in water overnight, this makes the most delicious, simple pudding you have ever eaten. In Ladakh they would not add sugar – I only do so here as the apricots we get are much less sweet.*

Simply soak the dried apricots overnight in the water and sugar, and enjoy in the morning.

CHULLI JAM

APRICOT JAM

MAKES 1 X 400 ML (14 OZ) JAR

INGREDIENTS

400 G (14 OZ) APRICOTS, WASHED, PITTED AND
ROUGHLY CHOPPED

200 G (7 OZ/SCANT 1 CUP) CASTER (SUPERFINE) SUGAR

JUICE OF 1 LEMON

Chulli (apricot) is the most popular locally grown fruit in the region, and beautiful apricot orchards can be found in different parts of Ladakh: in Sham Valley, the western part of the Indus valley, Nubra Valley and Dha-Hanu Valley. Various products are made from this delicious fruit, including dried apricots, apricot jam and syrups. Even the kernels are used, to make oil.

Place the roughly chopped apricots in a deep saucepan over a medium heat and cook for 10 minutes, stirring continuously. Add the sugar and cook for a further 20–30 minutes, stirring continuously, until the sugar is well dissolved and the mixture is sticky. Finally, add the lemon juice and cook for 5 minutes. Remove from the heat and leave to cool.

Pour into sterilised jars and seal. Unopened, the jam will keep for several months. Enjoy with a slice of toast.

GUR GUR CHA

BUTTER TEA

SERVES 3–4

INGREDIENTS

400 ML (13 FL OZ/GENEROUS 1½ CUPS) WATER

1 TEASPOON GREEN TEA LEAVES

300 ML (10 FL OZ/1¼ CUPS) MILK

½ TEASPOON SALT

1 TEASPOON YAK BUTTER (OR UNSALTED COW'S BUTTER)

Butter tea is the traditional beverage in Ladakh, also known as gur-gur cha. *Yak butter and salt are added to boiling water infused with tea leaves. The people of Ladakh drink butter tea every day. While visiting, I lodged at a farmstay and the lovely family kept refilling my cup with butter tea as soon I was finished. When I just couldn't drink any more, I kept hold of my mug until I was ready to leave. I was then told that their tradition is to keep filling the mug, but if you don't want any more, you must keep the cup full until you leave.*

Bring the water to the boil in a saucepan, then add the green tea leaves and boil for 30 minutes.

Strain the tea and return it to the pan, then add the milk, salt and butter. Bring back to the boil, then serve in small cups.

A LADAKHI LUNCH

The original plan for this trip was to travel by car from Srinagar to Leh, stopping in Kargil (Ladakh's second-largest town) to acclimatise to the altitude, before proceeding. However, the Zoji La (which translates as 'mountain pass of blizzards') lived up to its name. Thanks to heavy snowfall, it was closed to traffic. Instead, we booked a flight from Srinagar to Leh.

Dadul, who I had met on my last visit and who used to work for Sonam, had moved with his family from Leh to a village near the Pangong Lake. He is a clever, sharp and permanently happy man who is a delight to be around, and he joined us for our entire trip. We sat together having dinner at the Indus Valley Hotel in Leh, where I was staying, and planned the whole visit, deciding to stay relatively local.

One of my first stops was to meet two lovely sisters who are doing incredible things for the area: Tsezin Angmo, who runs Jade House, a homestay in Leh, and Kunzes Angmo, who runs Artisanal Alchemy food experiences, using Jade House as a base. It was their Ladakhi Lunch Experience that I was there to enjoy, with a menu that highlighted the food traditions and identities of their ancestors.

The climate of the Trans-Himalayan region is stark, so a robust diet was always required, historically rich in carbs, fat and, of course, red meat. It was exciting to see how the ingredients Kunzes cooked with differ from those used in other regions of India. In preparing her lunchtime feast, she used plenty of home-grown, organic dried fruits and vegetables; winter veggies that had been stored in root cellars; lacto-fermented vegetables (pickles); a great deal of local dairy, including dried cheese; and local and organic whole wheat and roasted barley flour, harvested from the family's ancestral fields and ground in a traditional watermill (*rantak*). Unusually for what most people know as 'Indian food', she used no turmeric (which, here, is used in traditional medicine but not in cooking), nor garam masala, red chilli powder or any masala at all. Traditional Ladakhi food, as she explained, uses only freshly ground black pepper and both fresh and dried herbs, such as wild chives, wild horsemint, coriander (cilantro), spring onions (scallions) and celery leaf, as well as yellow chilli for a hint of heat.

The menu Kunzes served was an incredible introduction to Ladakhi food – and the variety blew me away.

STARTERS

A platter of local breads and biscuits, served with a spread of sides and soup.

TSONG THALTAK

A wholewheat onion biscuit-bread, dressed with poppy seeds and traditionally baked in large, round, flat-lidded iron containers. Thes containers used to be buried in the dying embers of dry leaves and cooked slowly overnight, usually towards the end of autumn and before the arrival of spring.

KHAMBIR

A traditional sourdough loaf, made with local and organic whole wheat, leavened overnight.

BAZAAR E TAGI

A leavened flatbread, similar to Kashmiri *girdha*, which you'll commonly find for sale in old Leh. The name refers to the fact that this was the only type of bread sold at the markets, before modern commercial bakeries came into play.

ZATHUK (PAGE 216)

Also known as *zatshot thukpa*, this is a local wild stinging nettle soup, thickened slightly with *ngamphey* (roasted barley flour). It is seasoned with dried *tsong-lop* (spring onions), dried *tchin-tse* (Chinese celery), freshly ground black pepper and homemade white butter.

TANGTUR (PAGE 227)

A popular yoghurt dip that features foraged weeds and *saganik* (sometimes known here as sticky goosefoot or Jerusalem oak), seasoned with *oosu* (coriander), *phololing* (dried horsemint) and dried *skotse* (wild onion chives).

KHAGLA

Homemade cow's-milk butter.

LADAKHI ACHAAR (PAGE 235)

A local homemade vegetable pickle.

MAINS

Kunzes explained that she had chosen the main dishes she served to showcase the various influences on Ladakh's food identity over the years.

LAMA PAKTHUK

Meaning 'monks' *thukpa*', this is a dish made in monasteries, and particularly for monks visiting a household for ritual prayers. It is different from other *thukpa* – noodle soups that originated in Tibet – thanks to the shape of its whole wheat noodles/dumplings, and the fact that it includes non-sweet vegetables. Amongst the ingredients you'll find *churpe* (local dried cheese), *shranma* (dried black peas), julienned *nyungma* (turnips) and *gya-labuk* (Chinese radishes), as well as dried wild buckwheat leaves. The dish is seasoned simply with freshly ground pepper, dried Chinese celery, butter and coriander.

YARKHANDI PULAO (PAGE 232)

This dish travelled all the way from Yarkhand to Ladakh along the southern tributaries of the ancient Silk Road, and was a novelty decades ago, before rice was commonly available. The rice is cooked with big chunks of meat with plenty of fat, julienned local baby carrots, slivers of fried onion and aromatic whole spices, and is dressed with roasted nuts and black raisins. It is most similar to the Afghani and Mongolian pilafs.

CHUTAGI (PAGE 220)

A local creamy bow-tie pasta/dumpling dish, cooked with *tramnyung* (swede) – one of the vegetables most commonly used before German missionaries introduced potatoes to Ladakh in the 1880s. Shade-dried spinach and coriander are the added greens – and the dairy component in this and many other Ladakhi dishes is milk, unlike other parts of the country which tend to use paneer.

SKYU (PAGE 212)

Wholewheat pasta shaped like thumbprints, cooked in a meat-based gravy made with ground, organic sun-dried tomatoes. The stew also includes local swedes, is seasoned with coriander and black pepper.

LOKO-MOKMOK WITH SHA-PHING

Cup-shaped buns that were introduced to Ladakh by Tibetan refugees in the latter half of the 20th century. These particular buns are braised, rather than steamed, and soon after their introduction were replaced with *ti-mokmok* or *tingmo*, which are now synonymous with Ladakhi food identity. Kunzes served these *loko-mokmok* with *sha-phing* – a stew of mutton and rice noodles.

CHUTNEYS

THANGNYER

Not a Ladakhi delicacy as such, but a spicy chutney made with *thangnyer* (yellow Manali chilli), which is used rather than common red chillies to spice up Ladakhi food.

VEGETABLE CHATNI

A rustic mix of finely chopped vegetables – carrots, tomatoes, onions and coriander – spiced with yellow Manali chilli.

DESSERT

ORGANIC DRIED APRICOTS

Steeped in water overnight.

PAKTSA MARKU

Wholewheat dumplings cooked in butter and sugar, with added *chur-phey* (powdered dried cheese). Originally from Tibet, these dumplings are very similar in look to Tibetan *Bathuk*, Italian *cavatelli* pasta, or a more refined version of the Chinese *mao er duo* noodles.

The Artisanal Alchemy food experiences are tailor-made to cater to individuals' food preferences and tolerances, and are available at both Jade House and Ladakh's Stok Palace Heritage Hotel. They're a great way to gain an introduction to Ladakhi cuisine and food heritage – just be sure to pre-book! Once again, this was an experience I wouldn't have had without personal recommendations, this time from my chef friend Prateek Sadhu. I left with a recommendation from the sisters, too, who told me that I must visit Alchi Kitchen before leaving – somewhere that had also been recommended to me by my dear friend Sonal Ved, food editor at *Vogue*.

That evening, I returned to Charol's farmstay (page 210), grateful for the chance to catch up with her and her family once again. We enjoyed some delicious food and talked for hours, and I lamented the fact that COVID-19 had led to them temporarily closing their doors to overnight visitors.

BROKPAS &
ALCHI KITCHEN IN LEH

The following morning, we set off for Dha, or Dah village, which can be found on the way to Kargil. It was on this day that we made good use of the Protected Area Permits we'd had to buy. These permits allow foreign visitors to travel to inner line areas of the region, and must be purchased in advance. An early start meant that we stopped at Khaltse, around an hour and a half from Leh, for breakfast. Here, I enjoyed the best parathas I had eaten in a very long time – a meal that reminded me of my mum making her own incredible parathas for me and my friends, once upon a time.

The scenery along the Srinagar-Ladakh Road was so beautiful: for much of the route, we drove alongside the free-flowing Indus River, the bright white blossom of the apricot trees clearly visible on the mountains around us. We stopped several times to take photos of this landscape, which was unlike anything I'd ever seen – either in person or in pictures – anywhere else in the world.

Dha and Hanu are the only two Brokpa villages in Leh that are open to tourists. I'd been researching the Brokpa tribe for a while: although most of Ladakh's population is of Tibetan descent, the 2,000 or so Brokpas who inhabit the five villages in the Aryan Valley – known as the last Aryan villages in India – are Indo-Aryan in descent, and are said to be descended from a few members of Alexander the Great's army who settled in the region.

I was intrigued by the Brokpa way of living. Dadul asked some of the wonderful ladies we met if we could talk to them, and we were privileged enough to be invited into their homes, given tea and offered lunch – which we respectfully declined, still full from our breakfast en route. The meeting was an incredible experience: not only getting to know the people and their traditions and history, but also exploring their surroundings. As a chef and author, I would love to go back and stay a while to learn their cooking techniques and methods.

Tejis and her brother dressed for us in their unique and striking outfits, and shared more about their way of life. While much of Ladakh is Buddhist, Brokpas are Bonpos – they follow the Bon religion, indigenous to Tibet. This is a tribe in which it is not frowned upon for a woman to take more than one partner, and the fact that the Brokpas tend to marry within their community means that their distinctive looks – blue or green eyes and a fair complexion – continue to distinguish them from other Ladakhis.

As the ladies entertained us by playing the *sorna* or *sarna*, an ancient Iranian woodwind instrument, we learned that due to Dha and Hanu being lower in altitude than other parts of Ladakh, the average temperature is higher: there is far more greenery than elsewhere in the region, and the villagers are able to grow different crops. Apricots and apples are the main crops, with Tejis telling me that they commonly use the bitter kernels of the former to produce apricot oil. Throughout the area, depending on the time of year, you will also see walnut trees, cherry trees and wine grapes flourishing.

We had a few stops to make on the long journey back to Leh, the first being the Alchi Kitchen restaurant and cookery school. In late 2015, Nilza Wangmo gathered women of the community, both old and young, to document their recipes, before opening Alchi Kitchen the following year. Its remote location in this small lowland village may seem unusual, but Alchi Kitchen has been an incredible success story. Women travel from some distance to work with Nilza in her kitchen, and the place holds the accolade of being one of the first ever Ladakhi restaurants. Since it opened in 2016, Nilza has opened a second Alchi Kitchen in Leh and has been awarded the Nari Shakti Puraskar, a government award that celebrates the empowerment of women.

It is not just her care and love that have made Nilza's restaurant a success story, but her food, too. I completely fell in love with her cooking – traditional recipes that have been passed down from generation to generation – and enjoyed a feast of different dishes cooked by her and team: simple buckwheat pancake with walnut chutney, *chathuk* (made with millet and wild garlic), *saag*, *momo* dumplings and more. This place is a must-visit if you do ever venture to Leh.

Food devoured, we made our way to the nearby Alchi Monastery: a Buddhist monastery that is known as the oldest in Ladakh. This is far from a single building, though – it's actually an entire complex with four separate settlements, each of which dates back to a different period. The monastery dates back to either the 10th or 11th century, depending on which source you believe, but one thing is certain: its paintings are some of the oldest in Ladakh. Wander around, and you'll see some incredible wall art that combines both Buddhist and Kashmiri style, all housed within Tibetan architecture – it truly is an amazing place.

From here, we drove towards Nimmo to visit Sangam – the confluence of the Indus and Zanskar rivers. The sun was beginning to set as our taxi drove us towards the Sangam, and the deserted rafting station at Nimmo – the water levels in both rivers far too low for any rafting to happen. When the water levels are high enough (generally beginning in May), it's a popular pastime for rafters of all levels. I sat a while at the rafting station, watching the sun go down over the Indus River and admiring the changing colours of the water as the sunlight faded away.

RIGHT
Charol's mother-in-law, Palzes, with her granddaughter.

During the month of February, when the Zanskar River freezes, there is activity of a different kind: winter trekking. Known as the Chadar (sheet of ice) Trek, this ancient route has been used for centuries for both transport and trade and connects the villages of the Zanskar Valley, hidden deep within the mountains. February is the time when the ice covering the river is at its most stable – an important factor for those wanting to embark on an ice trek, the freezing cold water of the river rushing just a few inches below their feet. The danger is what appeals to many of the route's trekkers, who battle harsh conditions to make their way here and enjoy, one of the few – and relatively easy – trekking routes available in the region in the winter months.

About 25 miles from Leh, we stopped at the Gurdwara Pathar Sahib: a stunning Sikh temple built to commemorate the founder of Sikhism, Guru Nanak Dev and his visit to Ladakh. Sitting 12,000 feet above sea level, the Gurdwara houses an ancient boulder that features what is said to be the imprint of Guru Nanak, after a demon pushed the large rock down a hillside in an attempt to kill the Guru. As the rock approached, it softened and moulded into the Guru's back while he continued to meditate.

The following day was just as long, but just as important: I had been so looking forward to visiting the Pangong Tso lake, as I had been too unwell with altitude sickness to visit during my last trip. Situated on the Changtang Plateau in eastern Ladakh, the Pangong Lake sits 4,350 metres above sea level: a saltwater lake that is 83 miles long, five miles wide, and located partly in India and partly in China. From Leh, the drive took us around six hours thanks to the narrow, dangerous and icy road – it's certainly not a journey for the fainthearted!

I was excited that Dadul was joining us for this trip, as he is from this part of the country. He told us that many people choose to spend a night at one of the campsites on the banks of the lake, waking early the next morning to see some spectacular sunrises.

At one point on the journey, the photographer saw something flash across the road, and we quickly stopped to see if we could spot what it was. We were amazed to see an enormous Himalayan lynx, camouflaged within its surroundings, but staring directly at us. With Dadul declaring that he had never seen one in all his years in the region, it was a majestic sight that I felt incredibly lucky to see.

En route, we stopped at the Chang La: the second-highest mountain pass in the world at 17,668 feet above sea level, and one of the highest roads traversable by car in the world. Because of its altitude, it is advised that people spend no more than 25 minutes at the top – advice I heeded, as I did not want to get sick again! It was one of those experiences where you think to yourself, 'Did I really just do that?' I've never been an adventurous person by nature – my work has taken me to some incredible places, but I never thought I would experience anything quite like this.

Before leaving the main road to join the Pangong Lake Road, we stopped at Tangtse: a village that is a popular stopping point for those travelling this route. Dadul's cousin has a café here, where we enjoyed tea and a light breakfast before continuing our journey.

Normally an incredibly vivid blue in colour and a popular place for birdwatchers, thanks to its attraction to migratory birds, the lake was still frozen when we visited.

With news of the COVID-19 situation in India becoming worse and worse, the next day I travelled to Punjab to see my father before returning home. I was there for just one day before my husband contacted me to tell me that flights between India and the UK were set to be halted, so I immediately changed my flights, organised my COVID test and said my goodbyes. I always appreciate the time I do have with my dad (especially as it had been so long since the last visit, due to the pandemic), and he was excited to be able to cook a few things from my recent trip with me.

As I sat in my hotel room back in the UK, quarantining for the necessary period before returning home to my family, I reflected on my recent trip. It made me realise just how much more I still have to discover about the land that I call home: a realisation that makes me excited for future visits to India, but also a little sad. It was an important lesson that we can all learn from, especially when, thanks to COVID, our travel plans are somewhat restricted: no matter where we come from, how big the place is and how much of it we believe we know, there is always more to explore and learn about in our homelands.

THE END

ABOUT THE AUTHOR

Romy is a British/Indian chef, food writer, author and broadcaster. She was the owner and head chef at Romy's Kitchen. In 2016 she was appointed an MBE in the Queen's 90th birthday honours list. Romy is now one of the chefs on the new series of *Ready, Steady, Cook* on BBC One. She is a regular on *Steph's Packed Lunch*, and has appeared on BBC *The One Show*, *Country Life*, *Celebrity MasterChef*, *The Hairy Bikers' Comfort Food*, *James Martin's Saturday Morning*, *Sunday Brunch* and many more. Romy is also a regular on BBC Radio 4's Food Programme. She is the author of *ZAIKA: Vegan Recipes from India*, and regularly contributes to *BBC Food*, *Sunday Times* and *Telegraph* and international publications, including *The New York Times*. Romy was invited to speak at the Mad Symposium in 2018, and she has cooked at the prestigious James Beard Foundation in New York.

ACKNOWLEDGEMENTS

Without the help and guidance of Gundeep. Reet and Neev encouraged me to travel to these parts, to learn, share the knowledge of one's culture with the food.

Kajal Mistry, my wonderful publisher, this book would not have been possible without you believing in me. Thank you, and we need more publishers like you.

Mina Holland who taught me to write and gave me my first ever cook residency in the guardian, and Emily Knight who had encouraged me become to a better writer, and guide me every step when I doubted myself .

Chef Thomas Zacharias, who introduced me to Amit and guided me where to go.

Chef Prateek Sadhu guided me through the journey introducing me to many people along the way. Sadly, he was not able to make the journey due to COVID but I was lucky enough to meet his parents who were travelling to Kashmir. We had a long chat about food and their experience when they left Kashmir.

Amit Wanchoo – without him I wouldn't be able to meet the people and eat the food, cook or write the recipes. His mum cooked and shared many recipes with me, he took me to meet the *wazas,* and his team Salim and the driver, Younis, made my journey easy and comfortable.

Sanjoy Roy, for introducing me to his team which led me to meet the most wonderful lady Wafa from Café Liberty.

Roohi thank you for meeting and feeding me harissa and other dishes.

Wafa your passion and energy reminds me of me. Thank you for all the love you gave us each time I was there.

Hayat Bhat made time to treat me with the most delicious food at his restaurant Ahdoos. He also shared his recipes with me.

Ladakh wouldn't have been possible if Dadul didn't help me on both the trips.

He stayed me and took me everywhere I asked to visit. Dadul is friend for life

Charol and her family, for opening doors to me. Cooking with me and sharing their womdeful recipes with me.

Nilza Wango was introduced to me by the wonderful Sonal Ved. I had the most outstanding meal at her restaurant.

Sisters Kunzes and Tsezin Angmo – I had the most amazing lunch feast with them.

Evi O and Susan Le – my incredible designers. This book is beyond beautiful – I still can't get over the cover.

Poras Chaudhary, Matt Russell and Matt Inwood for their stunning photography. This book wouldn't have been possible without the three Musketeers.

Louie Waller, Nicole Herft and Simone Shagam for prop and food styling.

Tessa and Tim, my agents who believed in the proposal from the beginning.

Thank you to all the wonderful team at Hardie Grant: Emma Marijewycz, Eila Purvis, Emily-Preece Morrison, Laura Willis, Laura Eldridge Lorraine Woodcheke, Iman Khabl.

My handsome wonderful Dad, who is very proud of me for writing this book.

My sister-in-law Mandeep, who travelled with me to the unknown parts.

My sister Moni, and my niece Sofy made sure every day I was OK, as COVID was getting worse in India.

Ruth Wong, thank you for helping me raise a lot of money for different charities while writing this book.

Adele, I cannot thank you enough for helping me focus to write this book, and help me get back into the running again.

My neighbours, Natalie, Andy, Meg, John and Aurella for eating the food I cooked while testing the recipes.

Cooking with Dad at his house in Punjab, and trying out the recipes I was taught and given by various people on my journey.

Published in 2022 by Hardie Grant Books,
an imprint of Hardie Grant Publishing

Hardie Grant Books (London)
5th & 6th Floors
52–54 Southwark Street
London SE1 1UN

Hardie Grant Books (Melbourne)
Building 1, 658 Church Street
Richmond, Victoria 3121

hardiegrantbooks.com

Text © Romy Gill
Travel photography © Poras Chaudhary
Studio photography © Matt Russell

British Library Cataloguing-in-Publication Data.
A catalogue record for this book is available from
the British Library.

On the Himalayan Trail
ISBN: 978-1-78488-440-6

10 9 8 7 6 5 4 3 2 1

Publishing Director: Kajal Mistry
Editor: Eila Purvis
Design: Evi O. Studio | Evi O. & Susan Le
Photographers: Poras Chaudhary and
Matt Russell
Photo on page 204 © Matt Inwood
Food Stylist: Nicole Herft
Prop Stylist: Louie Waller
Copy-editor: Emily Preece-Morrison
Proofreader: Tara O'Sullivan
Indexer: Cathy Heath
Production Controller: Sabeena Atchia

Colour reproduction by p2d
Printed and bound in Italy by Rotolito

FSC
MIX
Paper from
responsible sources
FSC® C005461
www.fsc.org